ARCHITECTURE IN ASIA

ASIA NOW

ARCHITECTURE IN ASIA

ASIA NOW

WITH AN ESSAY BY DAVID N. BUCK

PRESTEL MUNICH · BERLIN · LONDON · NEW YORK

ASIA NOW

DAVID N. BUCK

The startling rise of new architecture in Asia over the last decade has been the most dramatic since the Industrial Revolution. This has been no watercolor dawn. More of a starburst! Driven this time not by post-war rejuvenation or by empire building but by economic development, architecture has been the symbolic vessel for national pride, individual aspiration, and collective success. The projects contained in this book are a celebration of this unique interaction of time and special locale. Asia is now the ground for innovation and icons: where else in the world could many of these buildings have been realized. This book looks at almost fifty projects that individually exemplify some of the most exciting architecture in Asia, and collectively explore the key issues that architects working in Asia face. Varying in scale from Power Unit Studio's single-family O House in Tokyo, to SOM's 88 floor Jin Mao Tower in Shanghai, they form a compendium of "local" projects, that explore universal themes. Does heritage always have to equal history? Can contemporary programs be fitted into traditional forms? How do foreign architects interpret local history? Why is the search for the iconic in architecture taking such prominence in these new constructs?

The buildings blocks of this story have been an alchemy of factors: firstly the economic rise of Asian countries, signified by the property boom in Japan in the late 1980s, has resulted in a dramatic shift of economic power and vitality eastwards. The six Asian countries reviewed in this book have a collective economy of 7,581,600 million dollars and a combined population of 1,532 million people. China is leading the charge: with an current annual growth of ten percent, its economy will double in size every seven years. Japan's Nikkei stock market index has doubled in value since early 2003, and even the slower growing economies of Taiwan and Malaysia are expanding at close to five percent. With growth rates like these, the Asian Tigers will soon be mammoths. This economic explosion has changed perceptions as well as the global marketplace. The speed of change is so fast now that the old definitions of "developed" and "developing" country no longer seem relevant: speed of change has overtaken level of attainment as the new barometer of success. And the process is ongoing. China's *per capita* GDP, currently ranked over 100 among the world economies, will grow rapidly over the next twenty years. As its economy makes great leaps forward, it will be combined with a low population growth: with more money spread over fewer people the Wild West's "heroic" expansion will seem like a backward country fair.

Secondly is urbanization. Although often perceived as having high population densities, the countries reviewed in this book diverge widely, from Singapore's 6,389 people per square kilometer, to China's 136. Even Japan, long viewed through the lens of crowded urban chaos, has a population density less than Belgium; China's half that of Germany. But the current process of urbanization is making huge changes. As people have moved away from an agrarian lifestyle, cities have been growing—both vertically and horizontally. The process of urbanization has been driven by technological, social, and economic changes, and for the first time in its history, the urban population of Asia now exceeds its rural one. These growing metropolises have been driven, typhoon like, by an internal momentum. Rather than temperature difference, new building has drawn in labor that then needs its own housing and infrastructure, and rising incomes have created an expanding middle class. This dramatic population move has also been driven in part by governments' desire for the retention of crucial agricultural land on the alluvial floodplains where many of these cities are located. This has inevitably led to a search for higher density, as well as taller buildings. A new juxtaposition is also taking place in the shadows of these buildings. Social divisions are spreading. The itinerant workers creating these towers are probably further away than ever from living in them themselves. Not just are the cities growing, so are the cracks in society.

Thirdly, there has been an ongoing search for icons to match the budding self-confidence and yet retain some national or ethnic identity. Architecture has benefited from being the most visible medium to structure this expression. Whereas in the Western Industrial Revolution many built symbols of pride had religious or community aspirations, much of the pride is now being expressed in more individual ways. Shopping and leisure are taking over from shared civic "duties," and so this new architecture has also, by default, traced an underlying social change. The group consensus has started giving way to individual exuberance, and this has infected architecture. Maybe that is why so many of the distinctive projects in this book are by Western architects. Not just do they have practical experience of building high, they also have personal experience of dreaming high. Their individual flights of fancy have become a means of codifiying and expressing collective pride, by cities, corporations, or entrepreneurs. This search for architectural identity can perhaps best be expressed as a numeric storm: a whirlwind of figures notating the story from architectural detail to city scale. There are 32,000 windows in Kuala Lumpur's Petronas Towers, and an 800 ton stabilizing bell inside the top of Taipei 101. China currently consumes forty percent of the world's concrete, and Prada's Tokyo store cost eighty-seven percent of Bilbao's Guggenheim Museum (Charles Jencks, in *Iconic Building*, p. 46). Beijing's proposed National Museum in Tiananmen Square will have a gross floor area of 170,000 square meters, the world's largest.

Within these unifying themes there are also enormous local variations. These six Asian countries encompass varied political, ethnic, and religious beliefs: China is a communist republic, but with fifty-five ethnic minorities. Singapore a democracy with multiple faiths from Hinduism to Taoism, Christianity to Buddhism. South Korea a republic with Shamanism accompanying Confucianism. And an equal diversity of geography and climate. What has been clear is that in spite of the regional variations, many of these projects, in addition to fulfilling programmatical briefs, have sought a wider symbolic resonance, seeking to communicate power, success, identity, or individuality. The search for iconic buildings is nothing new of course. The power of scale to dominate—think Great Wall of China—and image to convey—think Colosseum—has been known to both architects and commissioners of buildings since the Colossus of Rhodes. Many of the architects selected for this book have designed projects that seek not just international recognition but to interpret traditional ideas. In the last decade of Asian architecture three main motivic strands have started to appear to express this local identity.

VISUAL MEMORIES

The first is to use non-architectural symbols with a cultural or religious base. Renzo Piano's glass block boutique for Maison Hermès takes inspiration from *andon*, traditional Japanese lanterns that were carried in festivals. Part rice paper, part flame, they were objects that negotiated between the temporality of material and the permanence of fire. Perhaps Maison Hermès' translucent quality and luminosity doesn't just transpose the poetics of material from paper to glass, but also resonates between the transience of changing fashion and the permanence of desire. In neighboring Korea, Seoul's World Cup Stadium, built in 2002, derived its twin concepts of thin structure and translucent paper from traditional Korean artifacts of kites in the form of shields, and woven reed hats. Rendered in Teflon-coated membrane its unusual octagonal plan form not just reduced construction times and improved acoustics but also made passing reference to traditional Korean tableware. Built for the international focus that the World Cup brought to co-hosts Japan and Korea, the building tries to evoke both past and future visual memory. In China, the French architect Jean-Marie Charpentier's Opera House in Shanghai uses the square and circle, traditional symbols representing earth and heaven in Chinese culture. The traditional heavy-roofed hall of Chinese temples and palaces reconfigured into a large terraced steel roof with the glass clad sides allowing views past the foyers and boutiques to the 1,800 seat auditorium. These new buildings, devoid of traditional functions or—like Singapore's Assyafaah Mosque which uses a subdued symbolism of arabesque patterns to symbolize attributes of the Koran—facing the need for a less dominant representation in today's democratic times, have looked to unify identity around locally known symbols.

Sometimes reinterpreted through material change, sometimes through scale, they seek a bipolar identity: combining local evocation with a distinctive face to the "outside" world.

SENSUAL TOPOGRAPHY AND SYMBOLIC NATURE

The second is to use symbols and forces from the local environment. In China Paul Andrea's Guangzhou Gymnasium complex has three roofs that echo the organic curves of the surrounding hills. Appearing like a series of giant burial mounds, this sensual topography resonates with both the local landscape and yet uses the clarity of material to establish its contemporary identity. The Sail @ Marina Bay in Singapore uses the primordial forces of nature to sculpture two towers, honed symbolically by the natural forces of sun, wind, and water. With one tower 70 floors and the adjacent one 63, these twin residential towers billow onto the bay, glazed spinnakers on the harbor front of Singapore. Part man-made sculpture, part eroded canyon walls, they offer symbolic links in both directions—to human aspiration and natural forces. The 310-meter-high Menara Telekom Tower in Kuala Lumpur designed by Hiijas Kasturi Associates was influenced by the profile of the bamboo shoot. Considered a symbol of Malaysian identity, this metaphor was further developed in a series of "sky gardens" on every third floor where the outer "petals" of the building fold round—the cross section through a bamboo shoot reconfigured in glass and steel. Whereas in the past vernacular architecture used the materials of locally available nature to craft accommodation, these new interpretations express the locale through symbolic gestures. Removed from the constraints of local materiality through the use of new technologies, these buildings are free to return to the natural environment for inspiration, metaphor, identity, and sense of place. Structurally reinforced concrete, curtain walls, Teflon-coated membranes, and cantilevers—its not just spans that are increasing as these new materials create new expressive opportunities for architects.

SYMBOLS ON STEROIDS

The third strand is to re-work indigenous architectural motifs, reconfiguring the commonplace to create a new architecture of gestures to culture and aspiration. Argentian born Cesar Pelli used Islamic influenced geometry in the polygonal plan for the Petronas Towers in Kuala Lumpur. The twin towers, linked by a two-storey skybridge at the 41st floor, extruded the geometry of local buildings and details, into a 452-meter-high structure. Scale may have been extended, but the building's premise remained anchored to the local ground of geometric symbolism and cultural belief. The Jin Mao Tower in Shanghai quotes directly from the traditional tiered pagoda design, but again the scale is dramatically distorted. This building's atrium alone is 152 meters high, and spans 34 of the towers 88 floors. The tiered pagoda was also influential in Taiwan's Taipei 101 Tower, a staggering half-kilometer high. Like a Giacometti on steroids, its taunt astigmatism suspends optical belief and replaces it with dramatic symbolism.

But how do we evaluate this search for symbols? Perhaps the weakness of this appropriation of tradition is the emphasis on motivic development focused primarily on form. Whereas in music, augmentation and displacement, inversion and extension—forms of motivic development—give continuity to sonic themes, they are also underpinned by the serialism of extensive repetition. It is the continuity of motif rather than any individual "harmonic" resolution that gives legibility to the ideas and compositions. The isolation of many of these architectural interpretations of indigenous ideas may point to a significant weakness: while they work effectively in verbal client communication they may be less successful in urban communication. Certainly the chaos that strikes so many first-time visitors to Asian cities can not just be dismissed as an expression of local culture—it often also reflects a more centralized government approach that puts economic development above wider issues affecting quality of life. Cross-fertilization has been the ingredients of much innovation in Asian architecture through history, as buildings have expressed the language and cultural influences of the day. Some of these still remain. Japanese written language adopted the *kanji* ideographics from China and added their own phonetic pronunciation to the Chinese pronunciation. So these "Japanese" characters now contain both. Outside influences can be both incorporated and yet rebuffed in a process of cultural distillation. Of course it is not clear that physical stature on the skyline equates with an iconic building. Venturi and Scott Brown in *Learning from Las Vegas* argued—in the American context at least—that "big, high spaces do not automatically make architectural monumentality … and that we rarely achieve monumentality when we try" (p. 50). The last great comparable period of such architectural eclecticism that Asia currently enjoys was perhaps in nineteenth-century Europe. But here Venturi and Scott Brown argue that building styles corresponded to civic identity. So banks were classical basilicas to connote civic responsibility; universities used Gothic references to make symbols of the struggle of acquiring knowledge. What is interesting in the current context is that rather than meaning function, many of these new Asian icons strive for a bipolar message: emphasizing a universal corporate or city identity reflecting the globalization of the world economy, while stressing the genius loci of the native, the local, the indigenous. Taipei's Financial Center couples worldwide economic investment with the image of horticultural vitality. Kuala Lumpur's Petronas Towers for the Malaysian state petrochemical headquarters, utilizes an Islamic geometry for the plan, while incorporating designer Cesar Pelli's belief that buildings need foreground and background: foreground is the building's own exceptional qualities, background the urban fabric.

Why do so many designs work with isolated motifs? Certainly one part may be that the selection of non-Asian architects for many of these projects brings with it an inherent bias towards the obvious and identifiable. Perhaps even misunderstandings can give rise to new opportunities to redefine culture through the long distance lens. The architects helping to create this new renaissance represents a role-call of world talent. From Europe, Rem Koolhaas and Norman Foster, from America Kohn Pederson Fox Associates and SOM. The emphasis on form as the main method of communicating identity may result from the dramatic change of scale of many of these new buildings. Denied the materials and organization of vernacular architecture, as well as local precedents for their programs, perhaps the only element of indigenous architecture to translate has been gestures of form. Symbols have long been used in Asia of course to form marker buoys of identity. Japan's "rising sun," the heroic images from China's revolutionary "long march," the power

of symbols to crystallize a potent identity out of what has been a considerably intertwined past has long been recognized.

Unless of course, we shouldn't even be trying to emphasize local character? Japanese architect Hiromi Fujii has argued that his use of dislocated grids is not to deconstruct space or to reinterpret the modular basis of Japanese residential *minka* architecture, but rather to free the spaces from all cultural references. It is only then that we can experience them from an individual perspective. He argues that the repression of feelings by cultural expectation removed opportunities for genuine joy, fear, rage, intrigue. Individuality can only be found once the indigenous has been deleted.

ARCHI-EXTRAVAGANCE

What is clear is that modern architecture in Asia—while searching for local identity—is also producing spectacular technological innovations. Rem Koolhaas and his Office for Metropolitan Architecture's design for the Central Chinese Television (CCTV) Headquarters in Beijing is a three-dimensional puzzle, a continuous loop crisscrossed by a skin of structural members that render the structural forces onto the surface. Not only the building's form, but the structural expression provide contrasting scales and a distinctive silhouette: a new architecture where the rational premise of Modernism—that forms follows function, closely followed by detailing expressing structure—no longer applies. Meanwhile in Japan, Toyo Ito's flagship store for Italian designer Tod's has created a new evocation of nature. Situated on Omotesando street, the main tree-lined boulevard in central Tokyo, the building borrows both image and structure from the street's Zelkova trees. An arboreal-like reinforced concrete structure branches up from the street. The interstitial voids filled with a mix of aluminum and double-glazed polygonal panels are like crystalline gems where this architecture of nature asks questions about the future nature of architecture itself. The interplay between the luxuriant vegetation of the street and the building's contents is further intertwined at night, when the blackness of the Zelkova tree stems is echoed by the concrete structure. Light streaming from the boutique's interior cast shadows back onto adjacent buildings and trees themselves. It may finally be that rather than the current exuberance of form, that the lasting legacy of the new Asian architecture may be the development of new architectural and structural technologies.

Planning systems have allowed this diversity to take place. While years pass to gain permission for individual towers in central London for example, Shanghai now has over 2,000 skyscrapers (habitable towers over 152 meters high). In China, particularly with state-owned land and most development on seventy year leases, speed drives change. While the orthodoxy says democracy encourages diversity, maybe it also encourages restraint. There is an intriguing irony in centralized planning control actually resulting in pushing back boundaries, not pulling them in. So perhaps instead of thinking in terms of evolutionary change where by definition adaptations of individual species occur over a number of generations, we need to evaluate this architectural explosion more as a kind of spontaneous collective improvisation. Maybe its like a classic Miles Davis quintet, we need to look not so much at individual notes—or buildings—but more at the resultant collective composition.

FURTHER INTO THE FUTURE, FURTHER INTO THE PAST

As the old investment adage says, forecasting is always difficult, particularly about the future. But what can we anticipate for the next ten years of new Asian architecture? Three clear themes are developing. Firstly the continued development of new iconic architecture as cities continue to invest in their image and seek to establish their identity. This is bound to result in ripples out from the current cities into new hinterlands where the process of innovative architectural colonization can continue. With the next Olympics in Beijing in 2008, and the *Better City, Better Life* Expo in Shanghai two years later, continued innovations in form and structure will continue. This Expo will include two new convention centers as well as the world's tallest building in Kohn Pederson Fox's World Financial Center. Secondly, the search for a local identity for architecture will intensify. What forms and motifs, materials and organizations can best express long-held cultural beliefs, while encompassing future aspiration? There is no certainty that this needs to result in a "new vernacular." In Kyoto, probably Japan's most culturally conservative city, architect Shin Takamatsu saw his idiosyncratic Syntax and Origin buildings as similar to the first Chinese influenced temples that had landed amongst the *machiya* landscape first as alien forms, but subsequently adopted as Japanese. Finally the poetics of situation often conquers the dematerialization of symbol and form. Thirdly the other elements of cities, the open spaces, parks, and places for contemplation will be re-evaluated. There seems to be a universal trajectory for icons expressing collective success to be followed by the desire for individual quality of life. Asia over the last 50 years may have subjugated personal desire for collective advancement, but the next phase will be for public places for individual expression. In the way that Venice is defined by the Grande Canal, Manhattan by the Hudson River, and Rome by topography, no city can achieve iconic status in isolation from its environment. So environmental expectation will rise, and urban "culture" will be redefined to include the natural parameters as well as the man-made. The Japanese colloquialism for culture, *fu-do*, is after all a fusion of climate and earth. The environment has too often been the forgotten element in these cities. While rising land prices push open space off the agenda—and the site plan—the natural result of global climatic change will be felt most strongly in the densely populated urban coasts of Asia. The explosive growth of Shanghai, for example, has left the city subject to ground instability as high water tables—only 1,5 meters below the surface—have been distorted by the foundations of thousands of new buildings. While urban congestion and pollution rise, so will expectations of amenity. How ironic in many ways that as the information highway takes off and drives us towards a wireless future, that so much of Asian urban development is still being accompanied by highways of infrastructure and services. The open space opportunities inherent in the high-rise are being taken up by the support services needed to sustain them.

But one question that maybe in the end there is no need to worry about is how "Asian" the future architecture of this region will be. After all, the jazz pianist Bill Evans once termed the history question with a clear and simple view: that the person who sees furthest into the future also sees furthest into the past.

ASIA NOW

DAVID N. BUCK

Seit der Industriellen Revolution hat es keine derart spannende Entwicklung einer neuen Architektur gegeben wie die, die im letzten Jahrzehnt in Asien zu beobachten gewesen ist. Das war keine in Pastellfarben gezeichnete Morgendämmerung, sondern eher ein feuriger Sternenregen! Dieser Aufbruch ging nicht aus dem Neubeginn einer Nachkriegszeit oder der Demonstration imperialer Machtansprüche hervor, sondern aus einem stürmischen ökonomischen Aufschwung: Die Architektur war und ist das symbolische Ausdrucksmittel für Nationalstolz, individuelle Ambitionen und kollektiven Erfolg. Die beinahe 50 in diesem Buch präsentierten Projekte sind großartige Zeugnisse dieser einzigartigen Interaktion von Zeit und Ort. Asien ist heute der Boden für innovative und unverwechselbare Architektur. Wo sonst in der Welt hätten diese Gebäude realisiert werden können? Ob ein kleines wie das O House in Tokio, ein Einfamilienhaus des Büros Power Unit Studio, oder ein riesiges wie der 88 Stockwerke hohe Jin Mao-Turm in Shanghai des Büros SOM – jedes einzelne Gebäude stellt ein faszinierendes Beispiel für die neue Architektur in Asien dar, und zusammengenommen bilden sie ein Kompendium »lokaler« Projekte, die universale Themen behandeln und die wichtigsten Fragen verdeutlichen, mit denen die in Asien arbeitenden Architekten konfrontiert sind. Muss das Erbe immer der Geschichte gleichen? Können heutige Programme in traditionelle Formen eingefügt werden? Wie wird lokale Geschichte von Architekten aus dem Ausland interpretiert? Warum nimmt die Suche nach dem Unverwechselbaren eine so herausragende Bedeutung in diesen neuen Bauwerken ein?

Die Geschichte dieser neuen Architektur in Asien setzt sich aus den unterschiedlichsten Bausteinen zusammen: Da ist erstens der wirtschaftliche Aufschwung der asiatischen Länder zu nennen, der zu einer dramatischen Verlagerung ökonomischer Stärke und Vitalität in den fernen Osten geführt hat. Bezeichnend für diesen Aufschwung war der Immobilienboom im Japan der späten 1980er Jahre. Die sechs asiatischen Länder, die in diesem Buch zur Sprache kommen, haben zusammengenommen ein Bruttosozialprodukt von über 7,5 Billionen Dollar und eine Bevölkerungszahl von über 1,5 Milliarden Menschen. China stellt die Speerspitze dar; mit einem gegenwärtigen jährlichen Zuwachs von zehn Prozent wird sich die Wirtschaftsleistung des Landes alle sieben Jahre verdoppeln. Der japanische Nikkei-Index hat seinen Wert seit Anfang 2003 verdoppelt, und selbst Taiwan und Malaysia erreichen mit ihren sich langsamer entwickelnden Ökonomien noch eine Wachstumsquote von nahezu fünf Prozent. Setzt sich diese Entwicklung fort, werden aus den asiatischen Tigern bald Mammuts geworden sein. Diese ökonomische Explosion hat sowohl den globalen Markt wie auch die Wahrnehmungsmechanismen verändert. Die Dinge ändern sich heute so schnell, dass die Unterscheidung zwischen »entwickelten« und »sich entwickelnden« Ländern nicht mehr relevant zu sein scheint: Zum neuen Erfolgsbarometer ist – anstelle des Leistungsniveaus – die Entwicklungsgeschwindigkeit geworden. Und dieser Prozess setzt sich fort. Das chinesische Bruttoinlandsprodukt (BIP) pro Kopf wird in den nächsten 20 Jahren rapide wachsen. Und dieses enorme wirtschaftliche Wachstum geht mit einem geringen Bevölkerungswachstum einher: die denkbar besten Voraussetzungen für eine ökonomische Expansion, wie sie die Welt noch nicht gesehen hat.

Der zweite Faktor ist die Urbanisierung. Im Westen herrscht oft die Vorstellung vor, die ostasiatischen Länder seien alle sehr dicht besiedelt. Tatsächlich jedoch unterscheidet sich die Bevölkerungsdichte der in diesem Buch besprochenen Länder beträchtlich: von 6.389 Menschen pro Quadratkilometer in Singapur bis 136 in China. Selbst die Bevölkerungsdichte Japans – für viele der Inbegriff eines überbevölkerten urbanen Chaos – liegt unter der Belgiens. In Deutschland ist sie sogar doppelt so hoch wie in China. Doch der Urbanisierungsprozess, der in den letzten Jahren eingesetzt hat, führt zu gewaltigen Veränderungen. Immer mehr Menschen ziehen aus ländlichen Gebieten in die Städte, die sich sowohl in der Vertikalen wie in der Horizontalen ausdehnen; zum ersten Mal in der Geschichte übertrifft die städtische Bevölkerung in Asien heute die ländliche. Dieser Urbanisierungsprozess geht auf technologische, gesellschaftliche und ökonomische Veränderungen zurück, die wachsenden Metropolen werden wie ein Taifun von inneren Kräften angetrieben. Statt feuchter Luft saugen sie Arbeitskräfte ein, die dann untergebracht und versorgt werden müssen, und da die Einkommen steigen, bildet sich eine ebenfalls wachsende Mittelschicht. Diese dramatischen Bevölkerungsverschiebungen stehen dem Wunsch der Regierungen entgegen, das fruchtbare Schwemmland, auf dem viele dieser Städte angesiedelt sind, so weit wie möglich für die landwirtschaftliche Nutzung zu erhalten. Das führt zwangsläufig zu einer höheren Bebauungsdichte und höheren Gebäuden. Im Schatten dieser Gebäude entstehen neue soziale Spannungsfelder: Die Wanderarbeiter, die diese Türme bauen, haben wohl kaum die Aussicht, je selbst in ihnen wohnen zu können. Mit den Städten wachsen auch die Risse in der Gesellschaft.

Drittens gibt es eine anhaltende Suche nach sichtbaren, unverwechselbaren Symbolen, die das aufblühende Selbstvertrauen und auch – bis zu einem gewissen Grad – die nationale oder ethnische Identität zum Ausdruck bringen. Und welches Medium wäre besser geeignet als die Architektur, weithin sichtbare Symbole hervorzubringen? Während in der Industriellen Revolution des Westens der Stolz auf die eigene Wirtschaftskraft vor allem in symbolträchtigen kirchlichen oder öffentlichen Gebäuden zum Ausdruck kam, wird dieser Stolz heute vornehmlich in kommerzielleren, »privateren« Projekten vor Augen geführt. Shopping und Freizeitaktivitäten haben die »Gemeinschaftspflichten« in den Hintergrund gedrängt, der individuelle Anspruch ist an die Stelle des Gruppenkonsenses getreten, und dieser gesellschaftliche Wandel kann an der Architektur nicht vorbeigehen. Vielleicht ist das der Grund, weshalb so viele der unverwechselbaren Projekte in diesem Buch von westlichen Architekten entworfen wurden. Sie haben nicht nur die praktische Erfahrung, hohe Gebäude zu realisieren, sie haben auch die persönliche Erfahrung hochfliegender Träume. Ihre persönlichen »Höhenflüge« sind für Städte, Konzerne oder Unternehmer zu Ausdrucksmitteln kollektiven Stolzes geworden. Diese Suche nach einer architektonischen Identität wird vielleicht am besten anhand von Zahlen demonstriert, die Geschichten von einzelnen Gebäuden und von landesspezifischen Entwicklungen erzählen. Die Petronas Towers in Kuala Lumpur haben 32.000 Fenster, und in der Spitze des Taipei 101 befindet sich eine 800 Tonnen schwere stabilisierende Kugel. China verbraucht zur Zeit 40 Prozent der Betonproduktion der Welt, und die Baukosten für den Prada-Store in Tokio betrugen 87 Prozent der Kosten für das Guggenheim Museum in Bilbao (vgl. Charles Jencks, *Iconic Building,* New York 2005, S. 46). Nach der geplanten Erweiterung wird das Chinesische Nationalmuseum am Tian'anmen-Platz in Peking über eine Gesamtfläche von 170.000 Quadratmeter verfügen – ein Weltrekord.

Die Suche nach einer architektonischen Identität findet in den sechs asiatischen Ländern, die hier behandelt werden, unter Umständen statt, die sich in politischer, ethnischer und religiöser Hinsicht enorm voneinander unterscheiden: China ist eine kommunistische Republik mit 55 ethnischen Minoritäten. Singapur eine Demokratie, in der Hinduismus und Taoismus, Christentum und Buddhismus nebeneinander existieren, Südkorea eine Republik, in der der Konfuzianismus von schamanistischen Ritualen begleitet wird. Und ebenso groß ist die geografische und klimatische Vielfalt. Trotz aller regionaler und programmatischer Unterschiede haben viele der in diesem Buch präsentierten Projekte offensichtlich eines gemeinsam: Sie wollen eine breitere symbolische Resonanz erreichen, Macht, Erfolg, Identität oder Individualität zum Ausdruck bringen. Natürlich ist es kein neues Phänomen, mit Hilfe der Architektur Macht und Größe demonstrieren zu wollen. Seit dem Koloss von Rhodos haben sowohl Architekten wie auch Bauherren auf unverwechselbare Monumentalität gesetzt, um ihre Zeitgenossen zu beeindrucken – man denke nur an die Chinesische Mauer oder das Kolosseum. Viele der Architekten, die in diesem Buch vertreten sind, wollten mit ihren Projekten nicht nur internationale Anerkennung gewinnen, sondern auch traditionelle Ideen interpretieren, um eine regionale Identität zum Ausdruck zu bringen, und zur Erreichung dieses Ziels sind in der asiatischen Architektur des letzten Jahrzehnts drei Strömungen zutage getreten.

VISUELLE ERINNERUNGEN

Die erste dieser Strategien ist der Rückgriff auf »architekturfremde« Symbole mit einem kulturellen oder religiösen Hintergrund. Renzo Pianos aus Glasbausteinen erbaute Boutique für die Maison Hermès ist zum Beispiel vom *andon* inspiriert, einer traditionellen japanischen Festzugslaterne. Diese Lampen – teils Reispapier, teils Flamme – spielen einerseits auf die Vergänglichkeit des Materials und andererseits auf die Dauerhaftigkeit des Feuers an. Vielleicht überträgt die Durchsichtigkeit und Leuchtkraft der Maison Hermès nicht nur das Poetische des

Materials vom Papier auf das Glas, sondern stellt auch eine Anspielung auf die Vergänglichkeit der unbeständigen Mode und die Dauerhaftigkeit des Begehrens dar. Im benachbarten Korea wurde für das in teflonbeschichteter Membran ausgeführte Sangnam-Stadion, das für die Fußballweltmeisterschaft 2002 gebaut wurde, auf traditionelle koreanische Artefakte – schildförmige Papierdrachen und geflochtene Schilfhüte – zurückgegriffen. Die ungewöhnliche achteckigen Grundform half nicht nur, die Bauzeit zu reduzieren und die Akustik zu verbessern, sie verwies auch auf ein traditionelles koreanisches Teetablett. Als Austragungsort für die von Japan und Südkorea gemeinsame ausgerichtete Fußballweltmeisterschaft will das Gebäude sowohl die Vergangenheit als auch die Zukunft visuell erfassen und der Weltöffentlichkeit vor Augen führen. In China hat der französische Architekt Jean-Marie Charpentier für das Opernhaus in Shanghai auf das Quadrat und den Kreis zurückgegriffen, in der chinesischen Kultur traditionelle Symbole für die Erde und den Himmel. Das traditionelle wuchtige Dach chinesischer Tempel und Paläste wurde zu einem großen terrassierten Stahldach umgestaltet, und die Glasfassaden des Gebäudes geben den Blick durch die Foyers und Ladenlokale hindurch in das Auditorium mit 1.800 Sitzplätzen frei. Diese neuen repräsentativen Gebäude, die keine althergebrachten Funktionen erfüllen oder – wie die Assyafaah-Moschee in Singapur, in der mit Hilfe gedämpfter arabesker Muster der Koran symbolisiert wird –, sich in den heutigen demokratischen Zeiten bewusst zurücknehmen, greifen auf landestypische, mit neuen Materialien oder in andere Maßstäbe umgedeutete Symbole zurück, um sowohl nach innen als auch nach außen Identität zu stiften und der eigenen Bevölkerung wie auch der Weltöffentlichkeit ein unverwechselbares architektonisches Wahrzeichen vor Augen führen zu können.

SINNLICHE TOPOGRAFIE UND SYMBOLISCHE NATUR

Die zweite Strategie ist der Rückgriff auf symbolische Elemente und Kräfte der natürlichen Umgebung. Paul Andreus Sporthallenkomplex im chinesischen Guangzhou hat drei Dächer, die die organischen Wölbungen der umgebenden Hügel aufgreifen und an gigantische Grabhügel denken lassen. Diese sinnliche Topografie ist an die landschaftliche Umgebung angelehnt und nutzt zugleich der Klarheit des Materials, um seine Identität als moderne Architektur zu etablieren. Das Design des Wohnturmprojekts Sail @ Marina Bay in Singapur bedient sich der Urkräfte der Natur; die beiden Zwillingstürme mit ihren 70 bzw. 63 Stockwerken zeigen deutliche symbolische Spuren der Einwirkung der Sonne, des Windes und des Wassers und blähen sich wie verglaste Spinnaker über der Hafenbucht auf. Teils Skulptur von Menschenhand, teils nachgebildete Canyonwände, spielen sie sowohl auf die Gestaltungskraft des Menschen als auch auf die Kräfte der Natur an. Der von Hijjas Kasturi Associates entworfene 310 Meter hohe Menara Telekom Tower in Kuala Lumpur ist vom Profil des Bambussprösslings inspiriert, der als ein Symbol malaysischer Identität gilt. Weiterentwickelt wurde diese Metapher in einer Folge von »Himmelsgärten« auf jedem dritten Stockwerk, wo die äußeren »Blütenblätter« des Gebäudes sich falten – der in Glas und Stahl nachgebildete Querschnitt durch einen Bambussprössling. Während in der asiatischen Architektur der Vergangenheit heimische natürliche Baustoffe für Wohnhäuser verwendet wurden,

wird in diesen neuen Interpretationen der regionale Aspekt durch symbolische Gesten zum Ausdruck gebracht. Von den Einschränkungen der heimischen Materialien befreit, können diese Gebäude sich umso zwangloser von ihrer natürlichen Umgebung zu Metaphern mit einem Sinn für Ort und Identität inspirieren lassen. Stahlbeton, Vorhangfassaden, teflonbeschichtete Membrane und Auskragungen – die neuen Materialien lassen nicht nur neue Spannweiten zu, sie eröffnen den Architekten neue expressive Möglichkeiten.

KRAFTSTROTZENDE SYMBOLE

Die dritte Strategie ist die Hinwendung zu indigenen architektonischen Motiven, die Umgestaltung des Gewöhnlichen, um eine neue Architektur mit einem hohen kulturellen Anspruch zu schaffen. Für den polygonalen Aufbau der Petronas Towers in Kuala Lumpur hat sich der aus Argentinien stammende Cesar Pelli einer vom Islam beeinflussten Geometrie bedient, die zusammen mit anderen Charakteristiken der regionalen Architektur in die im 41. Stockwerk durch eine zweistöckige Himmelsbrücke miteinander verbundenen 452 Meter hohen Zwillingstürme eingegangen ist. Trotz seiner außergewöhnlichen Größe bleibt das Gebäude in der geometrischen Symbolik und der traditionellen Kultur des Landes verankert. Der Jin Mao-Turm in Shanghai lehnt sich unmittelbar an die traditionelle Form der gestuften Pagode an. Auch hier ist der Maßstab dramatisch gesteigert: Allein schon das Atrium des im Turm beheimateten Hyatt-Hotels ist 152 Meter hoch und dehnt sich über 34 der 88 Stockwerke aus. Auch auf den Taipei 101 in Taiwan übte die gestufte Pagode ihren Einfluss aus. Mit seiner atemberaubenden Höhe von einem halben Kilometer gleicht der Turm einer Giacometti-Plastik, die Anabolika geschluckt zu haben scheint.

Aber wie ist diese Suche nach Symbolen einzuschätzen? Die Schwäche dieser Traditionsaneignung ist vielleicht eine in erster Linie auf die Form konzentrierte motivische Entwicklung. In der Musik geben Vergrößerung und Übertragung, Umkehrung und Erweiterung – Formen motivischer Entwicklung – den Themen Kontinuität, sie sind zugleich von der Serialität einer ausgedehnten Wiederholung untermauert. Die Kontinuität des Motivs lässt die Ideen und Kompositionen lesbar werden, nicht eine individuelle »harmonische« Auflösung. Die Isoliertheit vieler dieser architektonischen Interpretationen indigener Ideen könnte auf eine signifikante Schwäche deuten: In der urbanen Kommunikation vermitteln sie sich längst nicht so erfolgreich wie in der verbalen Kommunikation mit dem Auftraggeber. Das für viele Besucher aus dem Westen verblüffende Chaos asiatischer Städte kann nicht einfach nur als Ausdruck der Lebensart der dort lebenden Menschen abgetan werden – oft zeigt sich darin die Auswirkung einer Politik, die der wirtschaftlichen Entwicklung Vorrang vor der Lebensqualität gibt. Die gegenseitige Befruchtung ist ein Wesensmerkmal der asiatischen Kulturen, und schon immer sind auch in der Architektur die sprachlichen und kulturellen Einflüsse ihrer Zeit zum Ausdruck gekommen. Ein Beispiel für die nachhaltige Einflussnahme einer Kultur auf die eines benachbarten Landes ist die japanische Schriftsprache. Die Japaner übernahmen chinesische Schriftzeichen – kanji – und fügten der chinesischen ihre eigene phonetische Lesung hinzu, sodass die »japanischen« Zeichen heute beide Aussprachemöglichkeiten bezeichnen. In einem kulturellen Destillationsprozess können Einflüsse von außen gleichzeitig aufgenommen und abgewiesen werden. Es ist natürlich fraglich, ob ein allein durch seine Statur eine Skyline beherrschendes Gebäude mit einem »ikonischen« Gebäude gleichzusetzen ist. Für Robert Venturi und Denise Scott Brown ist – zumindest im amerikanischen Kontext – »der große, hohe Raum nicht schon deshalb monumental. [...] Die Erzeugung von Monumentalität misslingt zumeist dann, wenn wir es gerade darauf abgesehen haben.« (*Lernen von Las Vegas*, Braunschweig 1979, S. 64). Die letzte große Periode eines architektonischen Eklektizismus, wie er zur Zeit in Asien zu beobachten ist, war vielleicht das 19. Jahrhundert in Europa. Venturi und Scott Brown zufolge entsprach damals der Baustil eines Gebäudes seiner bürgerlichen Bestimmung. Banken waren klassische Basiliken, um bürgerliches Verantwortungsbewusstsein zu suggerieren, die gotischen Elemente der Universitäten waren Symbole für Wissensdurst und Lerneifer. Interessanterweise wollen viele dieser neuen asiatischen Ikonen keine Funktion, sondern eine bipolare Botschaft zum Ausdruck bringen: Einerseits wird unter dem Gesichtspunkt der Globalisierung der Weltwirtschaft eine universelle Unternehmens- oder Stadtidentität hervorgehoben, andererseits der Genius loci, das Heimische, das Lokalspezifische, das Indigene. Das Taipei Financial Center verbindet weltweite ökonomische Investitionen mit einer Blumensymbolik. Die Petronas Towers in Kuala Lumpur, Zentrale des staatlichen malaysischen Mineralölkonzerns, greifen auf eine vom Islam beeinflusste Geometrie zurück und stehen gleichzeitig für Cesar Pellis Überzeugung, dass ein Gebäude einen Vordergrund und einen Hintergrund braucht: Die außergewöhnlichen Eigenschaften des Gebäudes sind der Vordergrund, das städtische Geflecht ist der Hintergrund.

Warum zeigen so viele dieser Gebäude isolierte Motive? Ein Grund ist sicherlich darin zu suchen, dass für viele dieser Projekte nichtasiatische Architekten ausgewählt wurden, und viele dieser Architekten haben eine Vorliebe für das, was offensichtlich und identifizierbar ist. Vielleicht können sich sogar aus Missverständnissen neue Gelegenheiten ergeben, kulturelle Phänomene durch den Blick von außen neu zu definieren. Die an dieser neuen Renaissance beteiligten Architekten repräsentieren die internationale Elite – aus Europa sind zum Beispiel Rem Koolhaas und Norman Foster vertreten, aus Amerika Kohn Pederson Fox und SOM. Dass Identität in erster Linie mit Hilfe der Form vermittelt wird, könnte seinen Grund in der Monumentalität vieler dieser neuen Gebäude haben. Die Architekten greifen nicht auf die Materialien und Konstruktionsformen der heimischen Architektur zurück, und da es in diesen Architekturen auch keine Vorbilder für ihre Entwürfe gibt, bleiben ihnen als regionale Architekturelemente, die sie in ihre Projekte übertragen können, möglicherweise nur Formgesten. Natürlich sind Identitätssymbole in Asien nichts Neues. Japans »aufgehende Sonne« und die heroischen Bilder von Chinas revolutionärem »langen Marsch« sind nur zwei Beispiele für kraftvolle identitätsschaffende Symbole, die aus einer komplexen Vergangenheit herausdestilliert wurden.

Ist es aber vielleicht sogar der falsche Ansatz, in der modernen asiatischen Architektur lokale Wesenszüge suchen und hervorheben zu wollen? Der japanische Architekt Hiromi Fujii hat behauptet, dass er mit seinen versetzten Rastern nicht den Raum dekonstruieren oder die modulare Grundlage der japanischen *minka*-Wohnarchitektur neu interpretieren, sondern die Räume von allen kulturellen Referenzen befreien will. Erst dann können wir sie aus unserer eigenen Perspektive erfahren. Ihm zufolge lässt die Unterdrückung von Gefühlen durch eine kulturelle Erwartungshaltung gar nicht erst zu, dass wir echte Freude, Angst, Wut, Neugier empfinden können. Eine eigene Perspektive ist erst dann möglich, wenn das Indigene eliminiert worden ist.

ARCHI-EXTRAVAGANZ

Es steht außer Frage, dass die moderne Architektur in Asien – auf ihrer Suche nach lokaler Identität – spektakuläre technologische Innovationen hervorbringt. Der Entwurf von Rem Koolhaas und seinem Office for Metropolitan Architecture für die Zentrale des China Central Television (CCTV) in Peking ist ein dreidimensionales Puzzle, eine ununterbrochene Schleife, die von einer Haut überzogen ist, die die strukturellen Kräfte auf der Fassade wiedergibt. Nicht nur die Form des Gebäudes, sondern auch der strukturelle Ausdruck bieten kontrastierende Größenordnungen und eine unverwechselbare Silhouette: eine neue Architektur, auf die die rationale Prämisse der Architektur der Moderne – dass die Form der Funktion folgt, dicht gefolgt von der Forderung, dass die Details die Konstruktion zum Ausdruck bringen – nicht mehr zutrifft. In Japan steht Toyo Itos Flagship Store für den italienischen Designer Tod's an der Omotesando, einer eleganten Allee im Zentrum Tokios, für eine neuartige Naturbeschwörung. Sowohl das Erscheinungsbild wie auch die Konstruktion des Gebäudes sind an die Zelkova-Bäume angelehnt, die den Boulevard säumen. Ein baumartiges Gebilde aus Stahlbeton wächst aus der Straße hervor. Die mit Aluminium und doppelverglasten polygonalen Fenstern gefüllten Zwischenräume gleichen Kristallen, in denen diese Architektur der Natur Fragen über die künftige Natur der Architektur stellt. In der Nacht, wenn die Schwärze der Zelkova-Baumstämme von der Betonkonstruktion aufgegriffen wird, wird das Zusammenspiel zwischen der üppigen Vegetation der Straße und den Gebäudeelementen noch enger. Das aus den Boutiqueräumen strömende Licht wirft Schatten auf die benachbarten Gebäude und Bäume. Als das nachhaltige Erbe der neuen asiatischen Architektur wird sich möglicherweise die Entwicklung neuer Architektur- und Bautechnologien herausstellen, und gar nicht so sehr der heute ins Auge fallende Formenüberschwang.

Ermöglicht wurde diese formale Vielfalt durch unbürokratische Baugenehmigungsverfahren. Während Jahre ins Land gehen, bis zum Beispiel die Baugenehmigung für ein einzelnes Hochhaus im Zentrum Londons erteilt wird, sind in Shanghai innerhalb weniger Jahre mehr als 2000 Wolkenkratzer (über 152 Meter hohe bewohnbare Türme) hochgezogen worden. In China, wo das Bauland für gewöhnlich dem Staat gehört und auf 70 Jahre verpachtet wird, treibt Geschwindigkeit den Wandel voran. Nach landläufiger Vorstellung fördert die Demokratie die Vielfalt, vielleicht fördert sie aber auch die Zurückhaltung. Es liegt eine verblüffende Ironie in der Tatsache, dass eine zentralisierte Planungskontrolle tatsächlich nicht zu enger gezogenen, sondern zu weiter gefassten Grenzen führt. Statt in Begriffen eines evolutionären Wandels zu denken – über mehrere Generationen hinweg werden einzelne Anpassungen vorgenommen –, müssen wir diese explosionsartige Entwicklung in der Architektur als eine Art spontaner kollektiver Improvisation betrachten. Wie bei einem Stück, das Miles Davis mit einem seiner

Quintette eingespielt hat, dürfen wir nicht auf einzelne Noten (Gebäude) schauen, sondern müssen das Ergebnis als eine kollektive Komposition wahrnehmen.

WEITER IN DIE ZUKUNFT, WEITER IN DIE VERGANGENHEIT

Ein altes Sprichwort der Investmentbanker lautet: »Vorhersagen sind immer schwierig – besonders wenn es um die Zukunft geht.« Was also können wir für die nächsten zehn Jahre von der neuen asiatischen Architektur erwarten? Drei Entwicklungen zeichnen sich deutlich ab. Erstens: Die Entwicklung einer neuen ikonischen Architektur wird sich fortsetzen; Städte werden weiterhin in ihr Image investieren und ihre Identität etablieren wollen. Dieser Prozess einer innovativen architektonischen Kolonisierung wird von den Städten aus ins Hinterland überschwappen. Die Olympischen Spiele, die 2008 in Peking veranstaltet werden, und die Weltausstellung, die unter dem Motto »Better City, Better Life« 2010 in Shanghai stattfinden wird, werden weitere formale und technische Innovationen mit sich bringen. Für diese Expo werden zwei neue Kongresszentren und mit dem World Financial Center von Kohn Pederson Fox das höchste Gebäude der Welt errichtet werden. Zweitens: Die Suche nach einer lokalen Identität für Architektur wird intensiviert werden. Welche Formen und Motive, Materialien und Ordnungen eignen sich am besten, um althergebrachte kulturelle Überzeugungen zum Ausdruck zu bringen und gleichzeitig in die Zukunft zu weisen? Das muss nicht unbedingt zu einem »neuen Traditionalismus« führen. In Kioto, der wahrscheinlich kulturell konservativsten japanischen Stadt, hat der Architekt Shin Takamatsu seine eigenwilligen Syntax- und Origin-Gebäude mit den ersten chinesisch beeinflussten Tempeln verglichen, die zuerst als Fremdkörper in der *machiya*-Landschaft aufgetaucht waren und später als japanisch angenommen wurden. Oft siegt die Poetik der Situation über die Entmaterialisierung von Symbol und Form. Drittens: Die anderen Elemente der Stadt, die offenen Flächen, Parks und Orte der Kontemplation, werden neu bewertet werden. Es scheint eine universelle Tendenz zu sein, dass auf ikonische Gebäude, die kollektiven Erfolg zum Ausdruck bringen, der Wunsch nach individueller Lebensqualität folgt. Wenn Asien in den letzten 50 Jahren die persönlichen Interessen der Menschen dem kollektiven Fortschritt untergeordnet hat, so werden in der nächsten Phase öffentliche Räume gestaltet werden, die den Menschen individuelle Ausdrucksmöglichkeiten bieten. Was wäre Venedig ohne den Canal Grande, Manhattan ohne den Hudson River, Rom ohne die Topografie der Stadt? Das unverwechselbare Bild einer Stadt wird von ihrer Umgebung mitbestimmt. Dieser Umgebung wird größeres Gewicht beigemessen werden, und die Parameter der Natur werden für die städtische »Kultur« genauso kennzeichnend werden wie die von Menschenhand geschaffen. Immerhin setzt sich der umgangssprachliche Ausdruck der Japaner für Kultur, *fu-do*, aus den Begriffen für Klima und Erde zusammen. Viel zu oft ist die Umwelt das vergessene Element in diesen Städten gewesen. Steigende Baulandpreise haben zu einer rücksichtslosen Dezimierung freier Flächen geführt – mit allen Auswirkungen auf eine menschen- und umweltgerechte Stadtplanung –, und die Folgen des globalen Klimawandels werden sich auf die dicht besiedelten Küstenregionen Asiens besonders deutlich auswirken. In Shanghai zum Beispiel hat das explosionsartige

Wachstum zu einer Bodeninstabilität geführt, da der hohe, nur 1,5 Meter unter dem Erdboden liegende Grundwasserspiegel durch die Fundamente Tausender neuer Gebäude in Bewegung geraten ist. Und mit der Überbevölkerung und der Umweltbelastung steigen auch die Ansprüche an die Lebensqualität. In mancherlei Hinsicht ist es schon ironisch: Während uns die Informationsautobahn in atemberaubender Geschwindigkeit in eine drahtlose Zukunft hineinführt, wird die städtische Entwicklung in Asien noch immer vom Aufbau einer modernen Infrastruktur begleitet. Die offenen Flächen, zu denen die Wolkenkratzer verhelfen könnten, werden von den Versorgungseinrichtungen in Beschlag genommen, die für die Funktionsfähigkeit dieser modernen Gebäude gebraucht werden.

Zum Schluss eine Frage, die sich von selbst beantworten wird. Wie »asiatisch« wird die Architektur der Zukunft in Asien sein? Der Jazzpianist Bill Evans hatte auf solche Fragen eine klare und einfache Antwort parat: Wer am weitesten in die Zukunft hineinschaut, schaut auch am weitesten in die Vergangenheit.

BEIJING

BEIJING

POPULATION EINWOHNERZAHL: CA. 15 MILLION INCLUDING THE GREATER
METROPOLITAN AREA INKLUSIVE METROPOLREGION
POPULATION DENSITY EINWOHNERDICHTE: 847 PERSONS PER KM²
AREA FLÄCHE: 16,808 KM²
WEBSITE: WWW.EBEIJING.GOV.CN

Beijing has been the capital of China for most of the past 800 years. Second only to Shanghai in terms of population size, Beijing ranks second among the top cities in China in terms of economic power and is first in terms of its investment environment. The municipality governs sixteen urban districts and two rural counties and covers nearly 17,000 square kilometers. The population of Beijing Municipality, which has tripled since 1949, totals fifteen million with a large but unknown number of migrant workers who reside without resident's permits. The permanent residents of Beijing come from all of China's fifty-six ethnic groups.

Peking ist seit 800 Jahren nahezu ununterbrochen Chinas Hauptstadt. In Bezug auf die Einwohnerzahl und die Wirtschaftskraft liegt die Stadt nach Shanghai an zweiter Stelle, doch nirgends wird derzeit soviel investiert wie hier. Die Stadt Peking besteht aus 16 Stadtbezirken sowie zwei Kreisen und erstreckt sich über annähernd 17.000 Quadratkilometer. Die Zahl der Einwohner hat sich seit 1949 verdreifacht und beträgt heute etwa 15 Millionen in der Metropolregion, nicht gezählt ist die große Zahl der Wanderarbeiter, die ohne Aufenthaltsgenehmigung im Stadtgebiet leben. Die registrierten Einwohner mit ständigem Wohnsitz decken alle 56 in China beheimateten Volksgruppen ab.

With a GDP growth rate of 9.1 percent, Beijing is steadily becoming more international and multi-functional. The city boasts the largest number of representative offices of foreign financial institutions while also attracting large investments from transnational corporations. So far, some 300 world-renowned corporations have registered 5,600 representative offices in Beijing, representing more than eighty countries and regions. Currently, Beijing is the country's largest science, technological, and cultural hub; the region has more than 400 national research institutes. Beijing is known to the world for its rich tourism resources and claims the most advanced infrastructure facilities in China.

Die Wachstumsrate des Bruttoinlandsprodukts liegt bei 9,1 Prozent. Peking wird internationaler und vielseitiger, kann die landesweit größte Zahl an Repräsentanzen ausländischer Finanzinstitute vorweisen und zieht umfangreiche Investitionen global agierender Unternehmen an. Ungefähr 300 renommierte Firmen aus mehr als 80 Ländern und Regionen haben insgesamt 5.600 Niederlassungen eröffnet. Darüber hinaus bildet Peking derzeit das wichtigste Zentrum des Landes für Wissenschaft, Technik und Kultur, die Stadt weist allein 400 nationale Forschungsinstitute auf. Peking ist weltberühmt für seine Vielzahl an touristischen Attraktionen und beansprucht für sich, die modernste Infrastruktur Chinas aufgebaut zu haben.

1 BEIJING'S OLD ARCHITECTURE IS BECOMING INCREASINGLY CRAMPED BY THE NEW.
PEKINGS HISTORISCHE ARCHITEKTUR MUSS MEHR UND MEHR NEUEN BAUTEN WEICHEN.
2 HEAVY TRAFFIC ON THE 3RD RING ROAD IN BEIJING.
DICHTER VERKEHR AUF DER 3. RINGSTRASSE IN PEKING.
3 BEIJING CITY DWELLERS PRACTICING TAI CHI CHUAN IN THE MORNING HOURS.
BEWOHNER PEKINGS BEI IHREN MORGENDLICHEN TAI CHI-ÜBUNGEN.
4 THE VIEW OVER THE ROOFS OF BEIJING.
AUSBLICK ÜBER DIE DÄCHER PEKINGS.

As host of the Olympic Games in 2008, the government of Beijing has launched a massive urban-renewal program. In anticipation of the event that is expected to attract 16.65 billion US dollars in direct investment and create 1.82 million new jobs, the city's economic and physical landscape has radically changed. Unfortunately, this immense urban growth has also had a negative impact. Many of the ancient, historical sites have been destroyed, to make way for apartment complexes, office buildings, and widened streets that are needed to accommodate the Olympic crowds. Other issues such as a dwindling water supply and increased inner city traffic are also becoming more acute; in 2005 there were 1,000 new vehicles on the streets every day.

Anlässlich der Olympischen Spiele, die 2008 in Peking stattfinden werden, startete die Stadtregierung ein umfangreiches städtisches Erneuerungsprogramm. Die Vorbereitung der Großveranstaltung, in deren Zuge man mit einem Investitionsvolumen von 16,65 Milliarden Dollar und 1,82 Millionen neuen Arbeitsplätzen rechnet, hat sowohl die wirtschaftliche Struktur als auch das Stadtbild Pekings grundlegend verändert. Das enorme urbane Wachstum wirkt sich jedoch auch negative aus. Zahlreiche alte, historische Stätten mussten neuen Wohnhäusern, Bürogebäuden und erweiterten Straßen Platz machen, die für die olympischen Teilnehmer und Besucher benötigt werden. Andere Probleme wie die Wasserversorgung oder die Verkehrssituation werden ebenfalls dringlicher: So wurden 2005 auf den Straßen täglich 1.000 neu zugelassen Wagen gezählt.

4

BEIJING BOOKS BUILDING

ARCHITECTS ARCHITEKTEN: **OFFICE FOR METROPOLITAN ARCHITECTURE (OMA)**
YEAR OF COMPLETION FERTIGSTELLUNG: **2008**
AREA FLÄCHE: **100,000 M²**

BOOKS GALORE

This extension and renovation of an existing cultural center by Dutch architect Rem Koolhaas and his team at OMA, the Beijing Books Building will be the largest of its kind in the world. Doubling its space to 100,000 m² the building will also feature a publishing and research business, film and television products, e-business and distribution service along with a platform for cultural exchange. An important new center for a city with sixty colleges and universities with over two million students, the new building is designed with a system of ramps that connect it to the existing structure. Instead of circulating customers through the building on escalators, the sales areas form a spiral movement of gradually sloping bookshelves that channel one through the building but also allow for browsing. The architects describe the facade as a "gigantic translucent bookshelf," allowing the building to "speak" of its function to the city.

BÜCHERWELT

Das Beijing Books Building, das durch die vom niederländischen Architekten Rem Koolhaas und seinem Team von OMA geplante Umformung und Renovierung eines bereits existierenden Kulturzentrums entsteht, soll das weltweit größte seiner Art werden. Die Fläche des Gebäudes vergrößert sich nicht nur auf 100.000 Quadratmeter, es wird auch um Forschungseinrichtungen, ein Medienbüro, eine E-Business- und Vertriebsabteilung sowie eine Plattform für kulturellen Austausch erweitert. Der Entwurf für den Bau, der als bedeutende Einrichtung der Universitätsstadt Peking gilt – es gibt 60 Hochschulen und über zwei Millionen Studenten –, sieht zahlreiche Verbindungswege zwischen Alt- und Neubau vor. Besucher werden nicht auf Rolltreppen durch das Zentrum geleitet; stattdessen ist der Verkaufsbereich spiralförmig angelegt, so dass man schmökernd und stöbernd entlang der ansteigenden Bücherregale wandern kann. Die Funktion des Baus wird auch nach außen transportiert: Die Architekten beschreiben die Fassade als »überdimensionales durchscheinendes Bücherregal«.

1 AT NIGHT VISITORS IN THE BEIJING BOOKS BUILDING APPEAR LIKE PIXELS ON THE FACADE.
NACHTS ÜBERTRAGEN SICH DIE BEWEGUNGEN DER BESUCHER IM BEIJING BOOKS BUILDING PIXELARTIG AUF DIE FASSADE.
2 THE TRANSLUCENT STACKED GLASS BLOCKS THAT MAKE UP THE FACADE.
DURCHSCHEINENDE GLASBLÖCKE BILDEN DIE FASSADE.
3 THE ARCHITECT'S VISION OF THE BUILDING BY DAY.
DIE VISION DES ARCHITEKTEN FÜR DAS GEBÄUDE BEI TAGE.
4 A RENDERING BY THE ARCHITECTS ILLUSTRATING CIRCULATION WITHIN THE CENTER.
DAS GESCHEHEN IM INNEREN DES KULTURZENTRUMS WIRD HIER IN EINEM RENDERING DARGESTELLT.

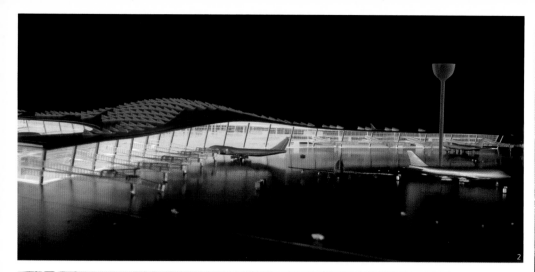

FLYING HIGH

Planned and built in just four years, the new terminal at Beijing International will make it the busiest in China. Designed by Foster and Partners, who were responsible for Hong Kong's Chek Lap Kok airport, it encloses an area of more than a million square meters and will accommodate forty-three million passengers per year, fifty-five million by 2015. Situated northwest of the capital with a cost of approximately two billion US dollars, visitors through this gateway to the 2008 Olympics will experience transfer times between flights that are kept to a minimum through extensive public transport, short walking distances, and daylit hallways that include a color orientation system. Southeast-orientated skylights—that maximize the heat gain of the morning sun—glow at night giving the terminal a sleek appearance. The sustainable design concept also sees the use of locally procured materials and skills.

HÖHENFLUG

Nach der Fertigstellung des neuen Terminals, der in einem Zeitraum von nur vier Jahren geplant und gebaut wird, ist der Flughafen von Peking innerhalb Chinas der Airport mit der höchsten Auslastung: Mit dem Terminal – entworfen von Foster and Partners, die auch für den Hongkonger Flughafen Chek Lap Kok verantwortlich zeichnen – werden auf einer Fläche von insgesamt über einer Million Quadratmeter 43 Millionen Passagiere pro Jahr abgefertigt, bis zum Jahr 2015 soll sich die Zahl sogar noch auf 55 Millionen erhöhen. Im Nordwesten der Hauptstadt gelegen, ist der etwa zwei Milliarden Dollar teure Flughafen nicht nur symbolträchtiges Tor zu den Olympischen Spielen 2008, sondern auch eine wichtige Drehscheibe; die Dauer der Zwischenstopps reduziert sich durch kurze Strecken, öffentliche Transportmittel und mit einem Farbleitsystem ausgestattete Verbindungswege auf ein Minimum. Nach Südosten ausgerichtete Oberlichter, die die Wärme der Morgensonne optimal in das Gebäude leiten, leuchten nachts und unterstreichen die elegante Erscheinung des Terminals. Das nachhaltige Entwurfskonzept sieht außerdem den Einsatz einheimischer Materialien und Bautechniken vor.

BEIJING INTERNATIONAL AIRPORT

BEIJING

ARCHITECTS ARCHITEKTEN: **FOSTER AND PARTNERS**
YEAR OF COMPLETION FERTIGSTELLUNG: **2007**
AREA FLÄCHE: **CA. 1,000,000 M²**

BEIJING INTERNATIONAL AUTOMOTIVE EXPO

ARCHITECTS ARCHITEKTEN: **HENN ARCHITEKTEN**
YEAR OF COMPLETION FERTIGSTELLUNG: **2007**
AREA FLÄCHE: **40,000 M²**

AUTO CITY

In good time for the Olympic Games in 2008 a permanent motor car exhibition, the International Automotive Expo, is currently being built in southwest Beijing and will bring together all global makes of car at a single location. The central, teardrop-shaped exhibition building invites visitors to take a journey that will lead them along several floors through the past, the present, and the future of the automobile. The endpoint of this trip will be a "University of the Motor Car," a research facility for technology and marketing. The exhibition building lies in a generously laid out park with artificial lakes and islands in which numerous glass pavilions—an echo of traditional Chinese garden design—offer additional useful floor areas. Automobile company buildings, car workshops, shopping areas, as well as hotels and congress centers complete the range of amenities offered by the car city.

AUTOWELT

Rechtzeitig zu den Olympischen Spielen 2008 entsteht im Südwesten Pekings mit der International Automotive Expo eine ständige Automobilausstellung, die alle globalen Marken an einem Ort vereint. Der zentrale, tropfenförmige Bau lädt auf mehreren Ebenen zu einer Reise durch Geschichte, Gegenwart und Zukunft des Automobils ein, an deren Ende sich eine »Auto-Universität« als Forschungseinrichtung für Technologie und Marketing befinden soll. Das Ausstellungsgebäude liegt in einem großzügig angelegten Park mit künstlichen Seen und Inseln, in dem zahlreiche Glaspavillons – eine Reminiszenz an die traditionelle chinesische Gartenkunst – weitere Nutzflächen bieten. Markenniederlassungen, Autowerkstätten, Einkaufsmeilen sowie Hotel- und Kongresszentren runden das Angebot der neuen Autostadt ab.

1 INSIDE THE TEARDROP-SHAPED EXHIBITION BUILDING VISITORS ARE OFFERED A TIME JOURNEY THROUGH THE HISTORY OF THE MOTORCAR.
DER TROPFENFÖRMIGE AUSSTELLUNGSBAU BIETET IN SEINEM INNEREN EINE ZEITREISE DURCH DIE GESCHICHTE DES AUTOMOBILS.
2 THE EXHIBITION FLOORS ARE ARRANGED IN A CIRCLE AROUND A CENTRAL ATRIUM.
UM EIN ZENTRALES ATRIUM SIND RINGFÖRMIG DIE AUSSTELLUNGSEBENEN ANGEORDNET.
3 AMONG OTHER FACILITIES THE FUTURISTIC BUILDING CONTAINS A "UNIVERSITY OF THE MOTOR CAR" FOR SCIENCE AND RESEARCH.
DER FUTURISTISCHE BAU BEHERBERGT UNTER ANDEREM EINE »AUTO-UNIVERSITÄT« FÜR WISSENSCHAFT UND FORSCHUNG.

CCTV HEADQUARTERS

ARCHITECTS ARCHITEKTEN: **OFFICE FOR METROPOLITAN ARCHITECTURE (OMA)**
YEAR OF COMPLETION FERTIGSTELLUNG: **2008**
AREA FLÄCHE: **550,000 M²**

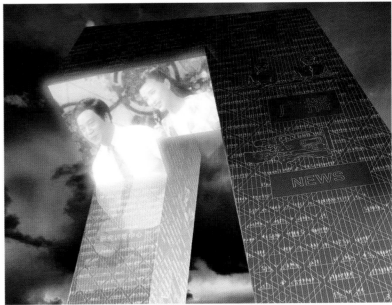

LOOKING INTO THE FUTURE

Due to be completed in time for the Olympics in 2008, this spectacular new 234 meters-high building for the headquarters of Central Chinese Television is set to replace the original CCTV Tower that was built in 1992 and that is the currently the tallest building in China. Consisting of two sloping 40 floor-high towers that are joined by a low L-shaped base and a cantilevered structure at the top, it will provide space for the entire process of television making from administration to broadcasting and program production for up to 10,000 employees. Including a hotel, a visitor's center, public theater, and exhibition spaces, Dutch architect Rem Koolhaas defines this looped building as a move away from the traditional tower to a "three-dimensional experience." Opposition to the projected building costs of 750 million US dollars has led to delays in construction and could see the opening moved to 2009.

BLICK IN DIE ZUKUNFT

Dieser spektakuläre neue Hauptsitz des Chinesischen Staatsfernsehens (CCTV) mit einer Höhe von 234 Metern wird den ursprünglichen Fernsehturm aus dem Jahr 1992 ersetzen, der momentan das höchste Gebäude des Landes ist. Die zwei schrägen, jeweils 40 Stockwerke hohen Türme, die durch L-förmige Bauteile an der Basis und an der Spitze miteinander verbunden sind, bieten Raum für die gesamte Fernsehproduktion des Landes, von Programmplanung und -sendung bis zur Verwaltung. Bis zu 10.000 Angestellte können in dem Fernsehhaus arbeiten, in dem es außerdem noch ein Hotel, ein Besucherzentrum, ein öffentliches Kino und Ausstellungsbereiche geben soll. Der niederländische Architekt Rem Koolhaas sieht in seinem Entwurf eine Abkehr von der klassischen Turmarchitektur, eine Wandlung zum »dreidimensionalen Erlebnis«. Widerstand gegen die geplanten Kosten von 750 Millionen Dollar führte zu Verzögerung der Bauarbeiten, so dass das Gebäude eventuell nicht wie geplant zu den Olympischen Spielen 2008, sondern erst 2009 fertig gestellt werden kann.

CHINESE MUSEUM OF FILM

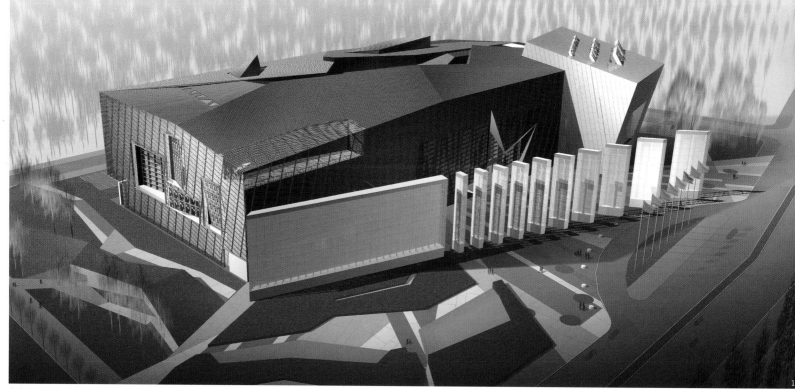

ARCHITECTS ARCHITEKTEN: RTKL IN ASSOCIATION WITH
BEIJING INSTITUTE OF ARCHITECTURAL DESIGN AND RESEARCH
YEAR OF COMPLETION FERTIGSTELLUNG: 2006
AREA FLÄCHE: 34,500 M²

ROLL!

The Chinese Museum of Film in Beijing marks the first time that a structure presents the entire cinematic history of China. On all four exhibition levels, offering 19,000 square meters of space, the visitor learns everything about the development of Chinese film and cinematic technique. Temporary exhibits are also planned. Additionally, the museum houses a 6,000 square meter large cinema complex complete with an IMAX theater, a large presentation room with 400 seats, three small rooms, and a multi-purpose hall. The thematic emphasis of the museum is reflected in its architecture—the structure resembles a clapboard, the ultimate symbol of the film industry. In front of the main entrance, as well as inside the museum, gigantic projection screens will be installed for the presentation of films.

FILM AB!

Mit dem Chinesischen Filmmuseum in Peking entsteht erstmals ein Haus, das sich ganz der cineastischen Geschichte des Landes widmet. Auf vier Ausstellungsebenen, die insgesamt eine Fläche von 19.000 Quadratmetern umfassen, erfährt der Besucher alles über die Entwicklung des chinesischen Films und Filmtechnik, außerdem sollen hier Wechselausstellungen eingerichtet werden. Darüber hinaus verfügt das Museum über einen 6.000 Quadratmeter großen Kinokomplex mit einem IMAX-Kino, einem großen Vorführraum mit 400 Plätzen, drei kleineren Sälen und einer Mehrzweckhalle. Der Themenschwerpunkt des Museums spiegelt sich auch in seiner Architektur wider: Die Form des Baus ist eine Anspielung auf die Filmklappe, das Symbol des Kinos schlechthin. Vor dem Haupteingang, aber auch im Inneren des Gebäudes werden zudem riesige Projektionsflächen für Filme installiert.

1 A BLACK, RECTANGULAR MAIN BUILDING AND INTEGRATED DIAGONAL PROJECTION SCREENS. THE MUSEUM HAS BEEN DESIGNED TO LOOK LIKE A DIRECTOR'S CLAPBOARD.
EIN SCHWARZER RECHTECKIGER HAUPTBAU UND DIAGONAL DAZU VERLAUFENDE PROJEKTIONS-FLÄCHEN: DAS MUSEUM IST EINER FILMKLAPPE NACHEMPFUNDEN.
2 SUPER-SIZED PROJECTION SCREENS IN FRONT OF THE MAIN ENTRANCE OF THE MUSEUM SET THE TONE FOR THE MUSEUM.
ÜBERDIMENSIONALE PROJEKTIONSFLÄCHEN VOR DEM HAUPTEINGANG DES MUSEUMS STIMMEN AUF DAS THEMA FILM EIN.
3 THE STRUCTURE'S EXTERIOR IS CLAD IN BLACK STEEL PLATING.
DER BAU IST AUSSEN MIT SCHWARZEN STAHLPLATTEN VERKLEIDET.
4 THROUGH THE EXTENSIVE ATRIUM, THE VISITORS HAVE ACCESS TO THE VARIOUS LEVELS.
DURCH EIN GROSSZÜGIGES ATRIUM HABEN DIE BESUCHER ZUGANG ZU DEN VERSCHIEDENEN EBENEN.

OPEN STRUCTURE

Located on a gentle rise in the center of the Olympic complex in Beijing, the National Stadium represents a new generation of sporting arena. The design, similar to a bird's nest, meets all the functional and technical requirements of an Olympic Stadium without confining itself to clichés. Estimated costs for the Stadium are around 500 million US dollars and when completed, it is believed that it will be the world's largest enclosed space. Facade and structure are one and the same; the building integrates facades, stairs, bowl structure, and the roof. Since all of the facilities—restaurants, suites, shops and restrooms—are self-contained units, it is possible to do without a solid, fully-enclosed facade. This allows for natural ventilation, which is the most important aspect of the stadium's sustainable design.

OFFENE HÜLLE

Das Nationalstadion, das auf einer sanften Anhöhe im Zentrum des Olympiageländes in Peking errichtet wird, steht für eine neue Generation der Sportarenen. Der an ein Vogelnest erinnernde Entwurf erfüllt alle funktionalen und technischen Anforderungen, ohne seine Einzigartigkeit einer herkömmlichen Stadionarchitektur opfern zu müssen. Die geschätzten Kosten für das Projekt, das nach seiner Fertigstellung den weltweit größten umbauten Raum bieten soll, liegen bei etwa 500 Millionen Dollar. Hülle und tragende Struktur sind eins, die Trennung in Fassade, Treppen, Dach und Stadioninneres nicht eindeutig. Alle zusätzlichen Elemente wie Restaurants, Logen, Geschäfte und sanitäre Einrichtungen sind als unabhängige Einheiten geplant, für die eine geschlossene Fassade nicht notwendig ist. Die offene Hülle des Stadions ermöglicht eine natürliche Luftzirkulation, was nicht zuletzt einen wichtigen Beitrag zur Umweltverträglichkeit des Baus darstellt.

1 THE 250,000 SQUARE-METER STADIUM IS BEING BUILT WITH 36 KILOMETERS OF UNWRAPPED STEEL, WITH A COMBINED WEIGHT OF 45,000 TONS.
DAS 250.000 QUADRATMETER GROSSE STADION WIRD AUS EINEM STAHLGERÜST MIT EINER GESAMTLÄNGE VON 36 KILOMETERN ERRICHTET, DAS ZUSAMMEN 45.000 TONNEN WIEGT.
2 THE STADIUM WAS CONCEIVED AS A COLLECTIVE VESSEL AND MAKES AN UNMISTAKABLE IMPRESSION FROM A DISTANCE AS WELL AS UP CLOSE.
DAS STADION IST SOWOHL AUS DER FERNE ALS AUCH IN NAHANSICHT UNVERWECHSELBAR UND EINDRUCKSVOLL.
3 THE SPATIAL EFFECT OF THE STRUCTURE IS NOVEL, YET SIMPLE; REFLECTING THE RANDOMNESS OF NATURE.
DER RÄUMLICHE EINDRUCK DES BAUS, DER AUF DEM ZUFALLSPRINZIP DER NATUR BERUHT, IST NEUARTIG UND DENNOCH SCHLICHT.
4 THE STADIUM HAS A CAPACITY FOR UP TO 100,000 SPECTATORS DURING THE OLYMPICS. THIS WILL BE REDUCED TO 80,000 AFTER THE GAMES.
DAS STADION KANN WÄHREND DER OLYMPIADE BIS ZU 100.000 BESUCHER AUFNEHMEN, DANACH WIRD DIE KAPAZITÄT AUF 80.000 PLÄTZE REDUZIERT.

NATIONAL STADIUM

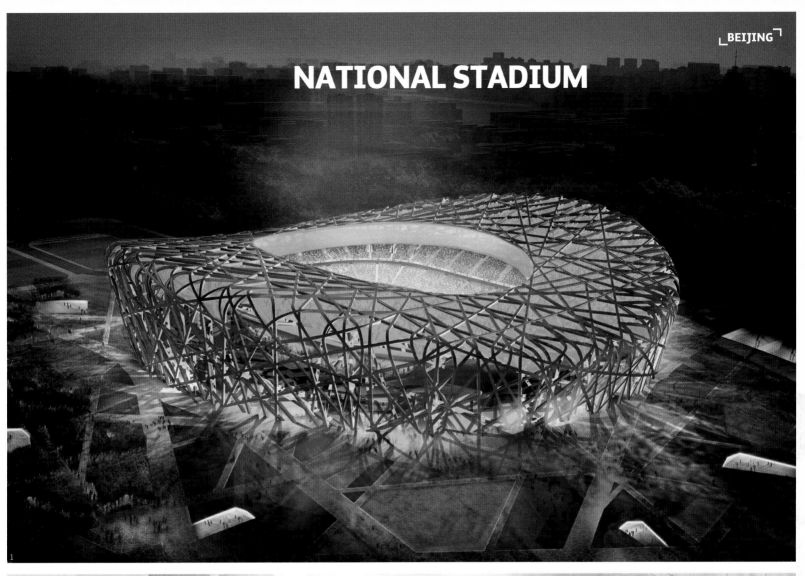

ARCHITECTS ARCHITEKTEN: **HERZOG & DE MEURON**

ENGINEERING AND SPORTS ARCHITECTURE TRAGWERKPLANUNG UND SPORTARCHITEKTUR:

CHINA ARCHITECTURAL DESIGN & RESEARCH GROUP, BEIJING; ARUP, HONG KONG AND LONDON

AREA FLÄCHE: **258,000 M²**

YEAR OF COMPLETION FERTIGSTELLUNG: **2007**

NATIONAL THEATRE

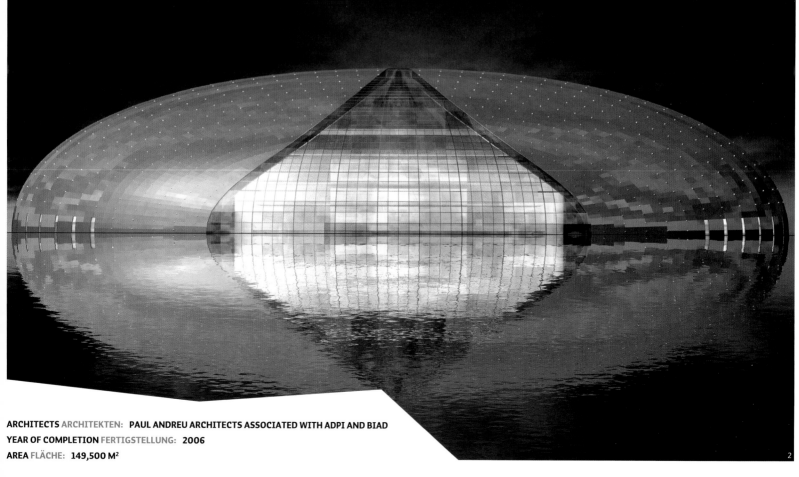

ARCHITECTS ARCHITEKTEN: PAUL ANDREU ARCHITECTS ASSOCIATED WITH ADPI AND BIAD

YEAR OF COMPLETION FERTIGSTELLUNG: 2006

AREA FLÄCHE: 149,500 M²

SHIMMERING DOME

An island of culture, in the truest sense of the word, sits upon an artificially laid lake in the heart of Beijing, only 500 meters away from Tiananmen Square: Paul Andreu's Chinese National Theater. Not only does it offer an opera house with 2,416 seats, a concert hall with 2,017 seats, and a theater with 1,040 seats, but also exhibition rooms, restaurants, and a large shopping area. The silver-gray ellipsical titanium dome is divided in the center by a narrow facade of safety glass, much like the opening of a curtain. The glass front allows for natural light during the day and offers the option of observing events inside the building, almost like watching a stage performance. The entrance to the National Theater is through a 60 meter-long transparent tunnel built under the lake. The structure seems to float on the water's surface without any anchoring or support.

SCHIMMERNDER DOM

Eine Insel der Kultur im wahrsten Sinne des Wortes ragt aus einem künstlich angelegten See im Herzen Pekings, nur 500 Meter vom Tian'anmen Platz entfernt: Paul Andreus Chinesisches Nationaltheater bietet nicht nur ein Opernhaus mit 2.416 Plätzen, einen Konzertsaal mit 2.017 Plätzen und ein Theater mit 1.040 Plätzen, sondern auch Ausstellungsräume, Restaurants und Einkaufszeilen. Der silbrig-graue ellipsoide Dom aus Titan wird in der Mitte durch eine Fassade aus Verbund-Sicherheitsglas wie ein Vorhang geteilt. Die Glasfront ermöglicht einerseits den Einfall von Tageslicht, andererseits kann nachts das Geschehen im Inneren des Gebäudes wie auf einer Bühne beobachtet werden. Der Zugang in das Nationaltheater erfolgt durch einen 60 Meter langen transparenten Tunnel, der durch den See verläuft: Der Bau scheint ohne erkennbare Verankerung oder Anbindung auf der Wasseroberfläche zu schweben.

1 SEEMINGLY INDEPENDENT OF ITS ENVIRONMENT, THE NATIONAL THEATER FLOATS ON AN ARTIFICIALY LAID LAKE.
SCHEINBAR AUTARK SCHWEBT DAS NATIONALTHEATER AUF EINEM KÜNSTLICH ANGELEGTEN SEE.
2 THE TITANIUM SHELL OPENS LIKE A CURTAIN. THE INTERIOR CAN BE SEEN THROUGH THE GLASS FACADE.
DIE TITANHÜLLE ÖFFNET SICH WIE EIN VORHANG: DURCH DIE GLASFASSADE WIRD DAS INNERE SICHTBAR.
3 THE VISITOR ENTERS THE STRUCTURE THROUGH A TUNNEL BUILT UNDER THE LAKE.
DER BESUCHER BETRITT DAS GEBÄUDE DURCH EINEN TUNNEL, DER UNTER DEM SEE VERLÄUFT.
4 BESIDES THREE THEATERS, THE NATIONAL THEATER OFFERS EXHIBITION ROOMS AND RESTAURANTS.
DAS NATIONALTHEATER BIETET NEBEN DREI BÜHNEN AUCH AUSSTELLUNGSRÄUME UND RESTAURANTS.

GUANGZHOU

GUANGZHOU

POPULATION EINWOHNERZAHL: CA. 9,400,000 INCLUDING THE GREATER
METROPOLITAN AREA INKLUSIVE METROPOLREGION
POPULATION DENSITY EINWOHNERDICHTE: 1,270 PERSONS PER KM²
AREA FLÄCHE: 7,434 KM² (METROPOLITAN AREA METROPOLREGION)
WEBSITE: WWW.GZ-GOV.ORG

Guangzhou, with its 9.4 million inhabitants living in the metropolitan area, is China's third largest city after Shanghai and Beijing. The capital of the congested Guangdong province consists of ten regions as well as two district-free towns covering more than 7,000 square kilometers.
Guangzhou ist mit seinen 9,4 Millionen Einwohnern in der Metropol-region nach Shanghai und Peking die drittgrößten Stadt Chinas. Die Hauptstadt der dichtbesiedelten Provinz Guangdong setzt sich aus zehn Bezirken sowie zwei kreisfreien Städten zusammen und erstreckt sich über mehr als 7.000 Quadratkilometer.

Due to its close proximity to the costal waters of the Pearl River delta, Guangzhou was long known as "China's Door to the World" and the financial and commercial hub of the Chinese market economy. Since 1957, the city biannually hosts the largest export trade fair in China, decisively facilitating its economic growth. Today Guangzhou boasts of the country's strongest economy behind Shanghai and Beijing. Its proximity to Hong Kong (132 kilometers) is also an important growth factor. Many multi-national companies have set up offices in Guangzhou, in fact, no other region, besides Shanghai, attracts more business travelers. The cost of living in the metropolis has lately toped that of the provincial capital Beijing.
Aufgrund der küstennahen Lage am Perlflussdelta galt Guangzhou lange als »Chinas Tor zur Welt« und Keimzelle der chinesischen Markt-wirtschaft. Seit 1957 findet hier zweimal jährlich Chinas größte Export-messe statt, die das ökonomische Wachstum bis heute entscheidend fördert: Mittlerweile hat Guangzhou nach Shanghai und Peking auch die stärkste Wirtschaft des Landes. Die Nähe zu Hongkong (132 Kilometer) ist ebenfalls ein wichtiger Wachstumsfaktor. Viele multinationale Un-ternehmen haben Niederlassungen in Guangzhou, keine Region außer Shanghai zieht derartig viele Geschäftsreisenden an. Die Lebenshaltungs-kosten in der Metropole liegen inzwischen höher als in der Landeshaupt-stadt Peking.

1 THE ZHUJIANG (PEARL) RIVER THAT PASSES THROUGH THE CITY.
BLICK ÜBER DEN PERLFLUSS, DER DURCH GUANGZHOU FLIESST.
2 SHANG XIA JIU SQUARE, A BUSY PEDESTRIAN SHOPPING MALL IN GUANGZHOU.
GESCHÄFTIGES TREIBEN IN DER EINKAUFSMEILE SHANG XIA JIU.
3 MANY OF GUANGZHOU'S RESIDENTS LIVE IN LARGE TENEMENTS.
VIELE DER EINWOHNER GUANGZHOUS LEBEN IN GROSSEN WOHNBLOCKS.
4 THE CITY'S ARCHITECTURE IS UNDERGOING RAPID TRANSFORMATION.
DIE STADTARCHITEKTUR BEFINDET SICH IN STÄNDIGEM WANDEL.

Like many large cities in China, Guangzhou has experienced a rapid architectural transformation in the recent past. The number of inhabitants has exploded and along with their growing wealth this boom has created the need for new—oftentimes exclusive—living spaces, greater leisure opportunities, better quality shopping, and the possibility to purchase international brands. Skyscrapers and shopping malls have been built, neon signs and reflecting facades line the streets. The city's desire to fit a cosmopolitan profile has lead to renowned foreign architects taking on various development projects—some examples are Zaha Hadid's design for an Opera House located in the new city center, Zhujiang, or the new TV tower in which ARUP and the Dutch office, Information Based Architecture, are involved.

Wie viele Großstädte Chinas hat Guangzhou in den vergangenen Jahren einen rasanten städtebaulichen Wandel erlebt. Im explosionsartigen Anstieg der Einwohnerzahl und dem wachsenden Reichtum einzelner Schichten gründet die Nachfrage nach neuem – zum Teil exklusivem – Wohnraum, nach mehr Möglichkeiten der Freizeitgestaltung, nach besseren Einkaufsmöglichkeiten und internationalem Markenangebot. Wolkenkratzer und Shopping Malls werden errichtet, Neonreklamen und spiegelnde Fassaden säumen die Straßen. Dem Wunsch der Stadt nach einem weltoffenen Profil entsprechend, werden Bauprojekte auch an renommierte ausländische Architekten vergeben – beispielhaft sind hier das neue Stadtzentrum Zhujiang, für das Zaha Hadid ein Opernhaus entwarf, oder der neue TV Tower, für den ARUP und das niederländische Büro Information Based Architecture verantwortlich zeichnen.

GUANGDONG MUSEUM

ARCHITECTS ARCHITEKTEN: ROCCO DESIGN LTD.
YEAR OF COMPLETION FERTIGSTELLUNG: 2008
AREA FLÄCHE: 60,000 KM²

OBJET D'ART

Rocco Yim's new construction, the Guangdong Museum, is expected to become one of Guangzhou's cultural landmarks. The design, created by the Hong Kong-based architects, relies on the idea that since a museum's structure serves as a casing for unique works of art, it too must seem just as precious. The building is inspired by Chinese lacquered boxes, which traditionally held valuables. Clean lines and flat outer walls incorporating openings of varying sizes, reminiscent of carvings, serve as an architectural antipole to the fluid forms of Zaha Hadid's Opera House, which will stand opposite the museum. Along with four large exhibition rooms, Rocco Yim's building offers space for administration offices along with exhibition related research and educational facilities.

OBJET D'ART

Rocco Yims Neubau des Guangdong Museums soll ein kulturelles Wahrzeichen Guangzhous werden. Der Entwurf des Hongkonger Architekturbüros basiert auf der Idee, dass ein Museumsbau, der als Hülle für einzigartige Kunstwerke fungiert, ebenso wertvoll anmuten solle. Das Gebäude ist von chinesischen Lackkästchen inspiriert, die traditionell der Aufbewahrung von Reichtümern dienen. Klare Linien und glatte Außenwände mit unterschiedlich großen Durchbrüchen, die an Schnitzereien erinnern, bilden darüber hinaus einen architektonischen Gegenpol zu den fließenden Formen des von Zaha Hadid entworfenen Opernhauses, das dem Museum gegenüber stehen wird. Neben vier großen Ausstellungshallen bietet Rocco Yims Bau Raum für Verwaltungsbüros sowie zu den Sammlungen gehörige Forschungs- und Bildungseinrichtungen.

1 THE BUILDING, IN THE FORM OF A JEWELLERY BOX, SURPRISES THE VISITOR WITH ITS NESTED INTERIOR COURTYARDS BEHIND ITS FACADE.
DER BAU IN FORM EINES »SCHATZKÄSTCHENS« ÜBERRASCHT HINTER DER FASSADE DURCH INEINANDER GESCHACHTELTE INNENHÖFE.
2 THE HEART OF THE EXTENSIVE MAIN HALL IS AN ATRIUM COMPLETE WITH AN INTERIOR POOL.
DAS HERZ DER WEITLÄUFIGEN HAUPTHALLE IST EIN ATRIUM MIT EINEM WASSERBECKEN.
3 IN THE EXHIBITION ROOMS, VISITORS CAN MOVE ABOUT FREELY FROM FLOOR TO FLOOR.
IN DEN AUSSTELLUNGSRÄUMEN KÖNNEN SICH DIE BESUCHER AUF MEHREREN EBENEN BEWEGEN.
4 THE ORGANIC FORMS OF ZAHA HADID'S OPERA HOUSE (LEFT) EXHIBIT AN EXCITING CONTRACT TO THE CLEAR-CUT LINES OF THE MUSEUM (RIGHT).
DIE ORGANISCHEN FORMEN VON ZAHA HADIDS OPERNHAUS (LINKS) BILDEN EINEN SPANNUNGSVOLLEN KONTRAST ZU DEN KLAREN STRUKTUREN DES MUSEUMS (RECHTS).

TEMPLE OF SPORT

Built for the occasion of China's ninth National Games in 2001, Guangzhou Gymnasium is one of the first internationally recognized architectural projects of the metropolis. Located in northern Guangzhou, the project links the urban density of the city to the un-developed, recreational area of the Baiyun Hills. The complex consists of three connected, clam-shaped buildings all in varying sizes. Each building is domed with white, semi-transparent plastic held taught by a lightweight steel construction that allows for natural, uniform light.

Next to the large stadium in the west section, that seats 6,500 to 10,000 depending on use, a trainings hall with a pool is housed in the center section while a public sports center can be found in the east section.

TEMPEL DES SPORTS

Das 2001 anlässlich der Nationalen Sportfest-spiele fertig gestellte Guangzhou Gymnasium zählt zu den ersten international beachteten Architekturprojekten der Metropole. Im Norden Guangzhous gelegen, stellt es ein Bindeglied zwischen der urbanen Dichte der Großstadt und dem unbebauten Erholungsgebiet Baiyun Hills dar. Die Sportanlage besteht aus drei zusammenhängenden muschelförmigen Bauten unterschiedlicher Größe. Jedes der Gebäude erhielt ein Dach aus weißem, halb-transparentem Kunststoff, der auf eine leichte Stahlkonstruktion gespannt ist und das Innere in ein gleichmäßiges Licht taucht. Neben dem großen Stadion im Westtrakt, das je nach Nutzung 6.500 bis 10.000 Sitzplätze bietet, beherbergt der Komplex im Mittelbau Übungs-hallen sowie einen Pool, im Osttrakt befindet sich ein öffentliches Sportzentrum.

1 THE INTERIOR LIGHTING OF THE STADIUM IS IDEAL FOR TELEVISION BROADCASTING.
DAS LICHT IM INNEREN DES STADIONS IST IDEAL FÜR FERNSEHÜBERTRAGUNGEN.
2 THE LIGHTWEIGHT STEEL CONSTRUCTION OF THE THREE-PART SPORTS COMPLEX RESTS ON A CONCRETE FOUNDATION.
DIE LEICHTEN STAHLKONSTRUKTIONEN DES DREITEILIGEN SPORTKOMPLEXES RUHEN AUF EINEM BETONFUNDAMENT.
3 THE HALF-TRANSPARENT CEILINGS GLOW IN THE EVENING EMPHASIZING THE ORGANIC QUALITY OF THE CONSTRUCTION.
NACHTS LEUCHTEN DIE HALBTRANSPARENTEN DÄCHER UND BETONEN DEN ORGANISCHEN CHARAKTER DER ANLAGE.

GUANGZHOU

GUANGZHOU GYMNASIUM

ARCHITECTS ARCHITEKTEN: **PAUL ANDREU**
YEAR OF COMPLETION FERTIGSTELLUNG: **2001**
AREA FLÄCHE: **100,000 M²**

GUANGZHOU OPERA HOUSE

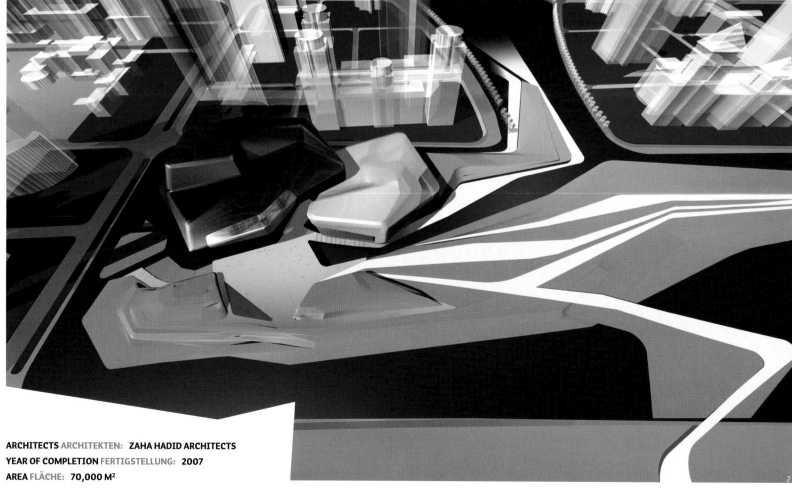

ARCHITECTS ARCHITEKTEN: **ZAHA HADID ARCHITECTS**
YEAR OF COMPLETION FERTIGSTELLUNG: **2007**
AREA FLÄCHE: **70,000 M²**

1 THE PROJECTED OUTER FACADE OF THE ROCK-LIKE BUILDING.
DER ENTWURF DER AUSSENFASSADE DES FELSENARTIGEN BAUS.
2 THE RENDERING SHOWS THE TWO AMORPHOUS VOLUMES AGAINST
THE BACKGROUND OF SKYSCRAPERS IN ZHUJIANG NEW TOWN.
DAS RENDERING ZEIGT DIE ZWEI AMORPHEN GEBÄUDETEILE VOR
DEM ENTWURF DES NEUEN STADTZENTRUMS ZHUJIANG.
3 THE MAIN AUDITORIUM TAKES UP THE UNDULATING FORMS OF
THE EXTERIOR AND WILL SEAT UP TO 1,800 PATRONS.
DIE GESTALTUNG DES HAUPTSAALS, DER BIS ZU 1.800 PERSONEN FASST,
GREIFT DIE WELLEFORMEN DES GEBÄUDEÄUSSEREN WIEDER AUF.
4 THE BUILDING WILL ALSO HOUSE A RESTAURANT, CAFÉ, AND
SHOPPING AREA.
DAS OPERNHAUS WIRD AUCH EIN RESTAURANT, EIN CAFÉ UND
EINEN EINKAUFSBEREICH BEHERBERGEN.

PERFECT FIT

Designed by Pritzker-prize winning British architect Zaha Hadid, Goungzhou's Opera House is situated adjacent to the new museum and library complexes on Zhujiang Boulevard and the riverside and dock area on the Pearl River. Taking up elements of Hadid's dynamic trademark style, this boulder-like building is composed of two amorphous volumes that form a kind of prelude to the Haixinsha Tourist Island Park beyond it. Seating 1,800 in its main auditorium, the fluid forms are continued inside the building that also contains a café, a bar, restaurant, and shopping area. An internal street cuts through the Opera House to meet up with the museum on the opposite side of the boulevard. VIP's have their own reserved entrance on the west side of the building on Huaxia Road.

ERSTARRTE MUSIK

Das Guangzhou Opernhaus der britischen Architektin Zaha Hadid, Gewinnerin des Pritzker-Preises, liegt gegenüber des neuen Guangdong Museums und der neuen Bibliothek am Zhujiang Boulevard, der entlang des Perlflussufers verläuft. Das an eine Felsformation erinnernde Gebäude, das Hadids dynamische Handschrift trägt, besteht aus zwei amorphen Baukörpern, die wie ein Auftakt zum benachbarten Haixinsha Tourist Island Park wirken. Die fließenden Formen der Außenhülle werden im Inneren der Oper fortgesetzt, in der neben einem 1.800 Personen fassenden Hauptsaal auch ein Café, eine Bar, ein Restaurant und ein Einkaufsbereich Platz finden. Für VIP-Gäste wird es einen separaten Eingang im Westteil des Gebäudes geben.

GUANGZHOU TV & SIGHTSEEING TOWER

ARCHITECTS ARCHITEKTEN: **ARUP AND INFORMATION BASED ARCHITECTURE**

YEAR OF COMPLETION FERTIGSTELLUNG: **2009**

FLOOR AREA FLÄCHE: **114,054 M²**

HEIGHT HÖHE: **37 FLOORS; ROOF** DACH: **454 M; ANTENNA** ANTENNE: **610 M**

1 RISING ABOVE ITS DENSELY SETTLED SURROUNDINGS, THE TOWER HAS A GRACEFUL, SCULPTURAL FORM.
DER TURM ÜBERRAGT MIT SEINER SKULPTURALEN FORM DIE DICHT BESIEDELTE UMGEBUNG.
2 THE INTERNATIONAL COMPETITION, HELD IN 2004, WAS OVER THE DESIGN OF THE TOWER, A 17.9 HECTARE PARK AT ITS BASE, AND THE MASTERPLAN FOR THE SURROUNDING 56.6 HECTARE AREA.
DER INTERNATIONALE WETTBEWERB, DER IM JAHR 2004 STATTFAND, RIEF AUF ZUR GESTALTUNG DES TURMES, DES 17,9 HEKTAR GROSSEN FERNSEHTURM-PARKS SOWIE DES 56,6 HEKTAR GROSSEN BENACHBARTEN AREALS.
3 THE NEW TOWER IS NOT ONLY A FUTURE ARCHITECTURAL ICON ON GUANGZHOU'S SKYLINE, BUT STANDS FOR THE ARCHITECTURAL BOOM IN CHINA IN GENERAL.
DER NEUE FERNSEHTURM GILT NICHT NUR ALS ZUKÜNFTIGES WAHRZEICHEN GUANGZHOUS, SONDERN STEHT FÜR DEN CHINESISCHEN ARCHITEKTURBOOM ALLGEMEIN.

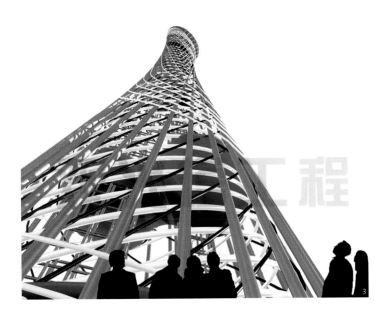

LOFTY TRANSMISSIONS

The TV tower currently under construction in Guangzhou will be the world's tallest. A collaborative effort by British firm ARUP and the Dutch architectural office, Information Based Architecture, outshone the international competition by creating a mega-structure with a human-like identity. The structure's twisted, freeform shape features a narrowing waist-line with a 180 meter-long open-air skywalk while the interior boasts a series of climate specific mini-buildings all strung together within a super-structure of glass and steel. A fusion between art and engineering, the tower is planned to attract 10,000 visitors daily with its TV and radio transmission facilities, observatory decks, revolving restaurants, computer gaming, exhibitions spaces, conference rooms, shops, and 4D cinemas.

FUSION AUS KUNST UND TECHNIK

In Guangzhou wird derzeit der weltgrößte Fernsehturm errichtet. Die britische Ingenieurfirma ARUP und das niederländische Architektur-büro Information Based Architecture gewannen mit ihrem Konzept eines Mega-Turmes mit anthropomorpher Anmutung den international ausgeschriebenen Wettbewerb. Die in sich gedrehte Konstruktion verjüngt sich auf halber Höhe zu einer Art »Taille« mit einem 180 Meter langen Freiluft-»Skywalk«. Das Innere der Superstruktur aus Stahl und Glas beherbergt als besondere Attraktion auf verschiedenen Ebenen eigens eingerichteten Klimazonen, vom Nordpol über die Tropen bis zur Wüste. Der Fernsehturm – eine Fusion aus Kunst und Technik – soll mit seinen Übertragungsstationen, seinen Aussichtsdecks, drehenden Restaurants, Ausstellungsräumen, Konferenzräumen, Geschäften und Kinos bis zu 10.000 Besucher täglich anziehen und gilt schon jetzt als Wahrzeichen des chinesischen Architektur-Booms.

HONG KONG

HONG KONG

POPULATION EINWOHNERZAHL: **7,041,000**

POPULATION DENSITY EINWOHNERDICHTE: **6,294.65 PEOPLE PER KM²**

AREA FLÄCHE: **1,103 KM²**

WEBSITE: **WWW.INFO.GOV.HK**

Located 60 kilometers east of Macau on the opposite side of the Pearl River Delta, the extremely important trade port of Hong Kong is one of the most densely populated areas in the world with over 6,000 people per square kilometer. Transferred from Britain to the People's Republic of China on July 1, 1997 it is made up of 236 islands in the South China Sea of which Hong Kong Island is the second largest and most populated. It is the fifth largest metropolitan area in the PRC. Largely made up of Cantonese Chinese, there has been a surge of immigrants from main-land China after 1997 with about 45,000 people per year settling in the city and increasing the development of Mandarin in the territory. Often described as a city where East meets West Hong Kong remains a massively popular shopping and entertainment haven for visitors from around the world.

Der Handelshafen von Hongkong liegt 60 Kilometer östlich von Macau auf der gegenüberliegenden Seite des Pearl River Delta. Mit 6.000 Ein-wohnern pro Quadratkilometer gehört diese Region zu den am dichtesten besiedelten Orten der Welt. Das Gebiet wurde am 1. Juli 1997 von Groß-britannien an die Volksrepublik China übergeben und besteht aus 236 Inseln im Südchinesischen Meer, von denen die Insel Hongkong die zweitgrößte und diejenige mit der größten Bevölkerung ist. Honkong bildet die fünftgrößte Metropolregion Chinas. Die Bevölkerung besteht zum überwiegenden Teil aus kantonesischen Chinesen, durch eine Ein-wanderungswelle vom chinesischen Festland kommen seit 1997 jedoch etwa 45.000 Menschen pro Jahr in die Stadt und erhöhen so den Anteil des Mandarin in der Region. Hongkong ist ein sehr beliebtes Einkaufs-und Unterhaltungsziel für Besucher aus aller Welt und wird oft als eine Stadt beschrieben, in der Osten und Westen aufeinandertreffen.

Hong Kong is the tenth largest and least restricted trading economy in the world. With over 123 foreign-owned licensed banks in the city, it has the largest external banking transactions volume anywhere. Its stock market is the third largest in Asia after mainland China and Japan. With growth rates of almost 10 percent in the 1970s and '80s, which slowed to the 3 percent range in the 1990s, especially after the Asian financial crises (and later the outbreak of SARS in 2002), the economy has stabilized with growth averaging 6,5 percent in 2005. The nominal per capita GDP of Hong Kong is slightly higher than that of the four big economies of western Europe namely: US$ 32,000. Along with Singapore, South Korea and Taiwan, as well as mainland China, its fast paced industrialization earned it place four as one of the four "East Asian Tigers."

Hongkong ist die zehntgrößte und eine der liberalsten Handelsnationen der Welt. Mit über 123 zugelassenen ausländischen Banken in der Stadt verfügt es über das größte Volumen an Banktransaktionen ins Ausland überhaupt. Der Aktienmarkt ist nach Festland-China und Japan der drittgröße Asiens. In den 1970er und 80er Jahren lagen die Wachstumsraten bei fast zehn Prozent, in den 90er Jahren sanken sie auf etwa drei Prozent, besonders nach der asiatischen Finanzkrise (und später dem Ausbruch von SARS im Jahr 2002). Inzwischen hat sich die Wirtschaft mit einem durchschnittlichen Wachstum von 6,5 Prozent im Jahr 2005 stabilisiert. Das nominale Bruttoinlandsprodukt pro Kopf ist etwas höher als das der vier großen westeuropäischen Wirtschaftsnationen, nämlich 32.000 US$. Zusammen mit Singapur, Südkorea und Taiwan sowie Festland-China zählt Hongkong dank seiner rasante Industrialisierung zu den asiatischen »Tigerstaaten«.

The majority of Hong Kong's citizens live in high-rise apartments. Few historical buildings remain in Hong Kong due to the city's almost manic urge to reinvent itself. Especially the area in and around Central has the tallest, most modern, and innovative buildings in the city. The Kowloon area, which did away with its strict height restrictions, will see a number of new skyscrapers and developments being realized there in the coming years. Architectural icons on its skyline are the 1990 Bank of China Tower by I. M. Pei, the HSBC Headquarters Building from 1985, as well as Norman Foster's Hongkong and Shanghai's Bank Headquarters from 1986. Currently the tallest building in Hong Kong is Two International Finance Centre which will be overtaken by the International Commerce Centre in 2007. Chep Lap Kok, Hong Kong's international airport near Lantau completed in 1998, was the city's largest and most extensive single civil engineering project to date.

Die Mehrzahl der Bewohner Hongkongs lebt in Hochhäusern. Aufgrund des beinahe zwanghaften Drangs der Stadt, sich selbst neu zu erfinden, sind nur wenige historische Gebäude erhalten. Besonders im und um das Stadtviertel Central stehen die höchsten, modernsten und innovativsten Gebäude der Stadt. In Kowloon, das seine strengen Höhenbegrenzungen abgeschafft hat, werden in den nächsten Jahren zahlreiche neue Wolkenkratzer und andere Bauvorhaben entstehen. Architektonische Wahrzeichen in der Skyline sind die Bank of China von I. M. Pei aus dem Jahr 1990, das Hauptquartier der HSBC von 1985 sowie Norman Fosters Hauptsitz der Hongkong and Shanghai Bank von 1986. Derzeit ist Two International Finance Centre das höchste Gebäude von Hongkong, es wird aber 2007 vom International Commerce Centre überholt werden. Chep Lap Kok, Hongkongs internationaler Flughafen in der Nähe von Lantau, der 1998 fertig gestellt wurde, war das bisher größte und umfassendste Bauprojekt der Stadt.

EMPORIO ARMANI

ARCHITECTS ARCHITEKTEN: MASSIMILIANO FUKSAS AND DORIANA O. MANDRELLI

YEAR OF COMPLETION FERTIGSTELLUNG: 2002

AREA FLÄCHE: 2,700 M²

RED THREAD

In its Hong Kong store the Giorgio Armani fashion group, best known for its exclusive purism, presents a new face. In an effort to utilize (interior) architecture to reach a younger age group catered for by the label Emporio Armani, the fashion designer commissioned Massimiliano Fuksas and Doriana O. Mandrelli, a duo who had already made a name for themselves with a series of innovative shops. At the centre of Hong Kong's financial district the new store offers a floor area of 2,700 square meters where customers can not only find the latest fashions but also a cosmetics department, a flower and book shop, and a restaurant. The theme of the interior design is movement. A "red thread," or more precisely an oversized band of glass-fibre reinforced plastic, winds in playful curves from the entrance through the restaurant to the sales areas, forming a decorative element here, a bar there, or even a DJ's console.

ROTER FADEN

Mit einem neuen Gesicht präsentiert sich das sonst für edlen Purismus bekannte Unternehmen Giorgio Armani in seinem Hongkonger Store: Um sich der jüngeren Zielgruppe des Labels »Emporio Armani« auch (innen)architektonisch anzunähern, engagierte der Designer das Duo Massimiliano Fuksas und Doriana O. Mandrelli, das sich mit einer Reihe von innovativen Ladenbauten bereits einen Namen gemacht hat. Mitten in Hongkongs Finanzdistrikt finden die Kunden auf einer Fläche von 2.700 Quadratmetern nicht nur die neuesten Modekreationen, sondern auch eine Kosmetikabteilung, ein Blumengeschäft, einen Buchladen und ein Restaurant. Das Thema der Raumgestaltung ist Bewegung: Ein »roter Faden« – genauer gesagt ein überdimensionales Band aus glasfaserverstärktem Kunststoff – läuft spielerisch verschlungen vom Eingang über das Restaurant bis zu den Verkaufsflächen und ist dabei mal dekoratives Element, mal Bar und mal DJ-Pult.

1 IN THE RESTAURANT THE RED BAND OF GLASS-FIBRE REINFORCED PLASTIC WEAVING ITS WAY THROUGH THE SPACE BECOMES A SURFACE TO LAY THINGS ON.
DAS ROTE BAND AUS GLASFASERVERSTÄRKTEM KUNSTSTOFF, DAS DURCH DIE RÄUME LÄUFT, WIRD IM RESTAURANT ZUR STELLFLÄCHE UMFUNKTIONIERT.
2 A STAIRCASE MADE OF STAINLESS STEEL AND PERSPEX CONNECTS THE DIFFERENT FLOORS.
TREPPEN AUS EDELSTAHL UND PLEXIGLAS VERBINDEN DIE STOCKWERKE.
3 BOTH THE COLOR AND THE INTENSITY OF THE LIGHTING CAN BE ADJUSTED.
FARBE UND INTENSITÄT DER BELEUCHTUNG SIND VARIABEL EINSTELLBAR.
4 THE ENTRANCE AREA PREPARES SHOPPERS FOR THE USE OF LIGHT AND COLOR AS DESIGN ELEMENTS.
DER EINGANGSBEREICH STIMMT AUF DIE DESIGNELEMENTE LICHT UND FARBE EIN.

1 UPON COMPLETION THE INTERNATIONAL COMMERCE CENTRE WILL BE HONG KONG'S HIGHEST BUILDING.
DAS INTERNATIONAL COMMERCE CENTRE WIRD NACH SEINER FERTIGSTELLUNG MIT 484 METERN HÖHE DAS HÖCHSTE GEBÄUDE
HONGKONGS SEIN.
2 THE TOWER WILL BECOME THE CENTER OF THE UNION SQUARE URBAN DESIGN PROJECT IN WEST KOWLOON.
DER TURM WIRD DAS STRAHLENDE ZENTRUM DES STÄDTEBAULICHEN PROJEKTES »UNION SQUARE« IN WEST KOWLOON.
3 THE NORTHERN ENTRANCE AREA OF THE INTERNATIONAL COMMERCE CENTER IS FLOODED WITH LIGHT.
DER NÖRDLICHE EINGANGSBEREICH DES INTERNATIONAL COMMERCE CENTERS IST LICHTDURCHFLUTET.
4 THE RESTAURANT IN THE TOP OF THE BUILDING OFFERS IMPRESSIVE VIEWS OF THE SKYLINE OF VICTORIA HARBOUR.
DAS RESTAURANT IN DER TURMSPITZE ERMÖGLICHT EINE EINDRUCKSVOLLE AUSSICHT AUF DIE SKYLINE DES VICTORIA HARBOR.

VERTICAL CITY

The International Commerce Centre forms
the heart of the Union Square urban planning
project that is currently being created around
a stop on the MTR (Mass Transit Railway) airport line. Upon completion the town will form
a kind of "miniature city" and its 118 floors will
contain not only offices but also numerous
shopping facilities, as well as an exclusive hotel
with 300 rooms, a wellness area, and swimming
pools. The hotel restaurant in the top of the
building will offer a spectacular view of Victoria
Harbor. The form of this building—that will
be one of the tallest in the world—is organic
yet at the same time elegant. At the base the
facade appears to peel away and extends on
three sides to form large canopy roofs.

VERTIKALE STADT

Das International Commerce Centre ist das
Herz des städtebaulichen Projekts »Union
Square«, das derzeit in West Kowloon um
eine Haltestelle der Flughafenlinie des MTR
(Mass Transit Railway) entsteht. Der Turm
soll nach seiner Fertigstellung eine »Stadt im
Kleinen« sein, und auf 118 Etagen nicht nur
Büroflächen bieten, sondern auch zahlreiche
Einkaufsmöglichkeiten sowie ein exklusives
Hotel mit 300 Zimmern, Wellnessbereich und
Pools. Das Hotelrestaurant in der Turmspitze
garantiert eine spektakuläre Aussicht auf den
Victoria Harbour. Die Form des Baus, der sich
in die Reihe der höchsten Gebäude der Welt
eingliedern wird, ist organisch und gleichzeitig
elegant. An der Basis scheint sich die Fassade
zu schälen und verlängert sich an drei Seiten
zu großflächigen Vordächern.

INTERNATIONAL COMMERCE CENTRE

ARCHITECTS ARCHITEKTEN: **KOHN PEDERSEN FOX ASSOCIATES**
YEAR OF COMPLETION FERTIGSTELLUNG: **2010**
AREA FLÄCHE: **270,000 M²**
HEIGHT HÖHE: **484 M**

HONG KONG'S TALLEST

Like the Jin Mao Tower in Shanghai this shimmering beacon near Victoria Harbour, built in just three years, has 88 floors, a lucky number in Chinese culture. With its 415 meters it is as high as the former South Tower of the World Trade Center in New York and will be the highest building in the city until the completion of the International Commerce Centre in 2007. Built to withstand typhoons, the center can accommodate up to 15,000 people, is equipped with double-deck elevators, houses the Four Seasons hotel in Hong Kong as well as offices for major international finance firms, and has a mall that features fashion, jewelry, and grocery stores along with restaurants and a cinema. The floors are raised for flexible cable management, while the floor plans are almost column free. On the 55th floor the public viewing platform affords visitors astounding views over the city.

HONGKONGS GRÖSSTER

Wie auch der Jin Mao Tower in Shanghai hat dieses schimmernde Wahrzeichen in der Nähe des Victoria Harbour 88 Stockwerke, eine Glückszahl in der chinesischen Kultur. Der in nur drei Jahren erbaute Turm erreicht mit seinen 415 Metern die gleiche Höhe wie der ehemalige Südturm des World Trade Centers in New York und wird bis zur Fertigstellung des International Commerce Centre im Jahr 2007 das höchste Gebäude der Stadt sein. Die Konstruktion ist darauf ausgerichtet, Taifunen standzuhalten. Der Turm verfügt über Doppelstockaufzüge für die bis zu 15.000 Menschen, die in dem Gebäude Platz finden, und beherbergt neben dem Hotel Four Seasons auch Büroräumen wichtiger internationaler Finanzunternehmen sowie ein Einkaufszentrum mit Mode-, Schmuck- und Lebensmittelgeschäften, Restaurants und einem Kino. Die Stockwerke sind erhöht, um eine flexible Verlegung der Leitungen zu ermöglichen, die Grundrisse sind nahezu stützenfrei. Im 55. Stock bietet die Aussichtsplattform Besuchern beeindruckende Ausblicke über die Stadt.

TWO INTERNATIONAL FINANCE CENTRE

ARCHITECTS ARCHITEKTEN: **CESAR PELLI & ASSOCIATES**
YEAR OF COMPLETION FERTIGSTELLUNG: **2003**
AREA FLÄCHE: **185,805 M²**

WEST KOWLOON CULTURAL DISTRICT

ARCHITECTS ARCHITEKTEN: **FOSTER AND PARTNERS**
YEAR OF COMPLETION FERTIGSTELLUNG: **2011**
AREA FLÄCHE: **100 ACRES** 40 HEKTAR

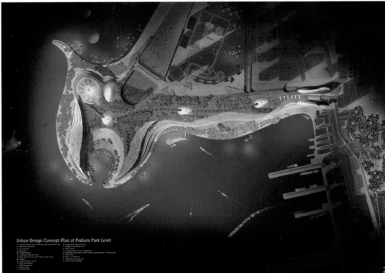

FROM COMMERCE TO CULTURE

One of the biggest projects currently under development directly opposite Hong Kong Island is the Cultural District on the reclaimed land of the West Kowloon waterfront. Designed by Norman Foster who also designed the iconic Hongkong and Shanghai Bank headquarters in 1986, the development is to consolidate the city's reputation as a cultural destination. A massive multi-floored canopy will envelope a number of venues for the arts including theater and concert halls, a museum along with cinemas, restaurants, shops, and an extensive urban park. Apart from merely providing shelter from the elements the canopy is designed to create a comfortable micro-climate for visitors while an advanced transportation system linked with that from the city allows for easy movement to the various venues. The realization of the project has been delayed due to the proposed high costs involved and differences of opinion between developers and the government.

VOM HANDEL ZUR KULTUR

Eines der derzeit größten Bauvorhaben ist das direkt gegenüber der Insel Hongkong gelegene Kulturviertel, das auf dem künstlich aufgeschütteten Land am Ufer von West Kowloon entstehen wird. Der Entwurf stammt von Norman Foster, der auch den Hauptsitz der Hongkong and Shanghai Bank 1986 entworfen hat, und soll den Ruf der Stadt als Kulturmetropole fördern. Unter einem gewaltigen gewölbten Dach wird eine Anzahl von Veranstaltungsorten Platz finden, darunter Theater- und Konzertsäle, ein Museum sowie Kinos, Restaurants, Geschäfte und ein weitläufiger städtischer Park. Dabei bietet das Dach nicht nur Schutz vor den Elementen, es ist auch so konstruiert, dass es für die Besucher ein angenehmes Mikroklima schafft. Ein hochentwickeltes Transportsystem, das mit dem der Stadt verbunden ist, erlaubt eine bequeme Fortbewegung zwischen den einzelnen Veranstaltungsorten. Die Ausführung des Projekts wurde durch die hohen geplanten Kosten und Unstimmigkeiten zwischen dem Bauträger und der Regierung verzögert.

1 A RENDERING BY THE ARCHITECTS SHOWING THE PROPOSED DEVELOPMENT AGAINST THE MULTITUDE OF HONG KONG'S SKYSCRAPERS.
EIN RENDERING DER ARCHITEKTEN ZEIGT DAS BAUVORHABEN VOR DEN WOLKENKRATZERN HONGKONGS.
2 THE FORM OF THE CANOPY WAS INSPIRED BY THE TOPOGRAPHY OF HONG KONG'S PENINSULA.
DIE FORM DES GEWÖLBTEN DACHS WURDE VON DER TOPOGRAPHIE DER HALBINSEL HONGKONG ANGEREGT.
3 COVERING OVER 100 ACRES IN LAND 70 PERCENT OF THE SITE IS GIVEN OVER TO PARKLAND.
AUF 70 PROZENT DER ÜBER 40 HEKTAR GROSSEN FLÄCHE WIRD EIN PARK ENTSTEHEN.

KUALA LUMPUR

KUALA LUMPUR

POPULATION EINWOHNERZAHL: CA. 1.5 MILLION; MORE THAN 4 MILLION
IN THE METROPOLITAN AREA METROPOLREGION
POPULATION DENSITY EINWOHNERDICHTE: 4,621 PERSONS PER KM²
AREA FLÄCHE: 243 KM²

Kuala Lumpur, which was founded in 1857 by tin miners, lies in the south of the Malay Peninsula on the Rivers Gombak and Kelang. Today it is Malaysia's largest city, the capital and the main cultural centre. The urban population is made up of different ethnic groups: 52 percent Chinese, 39 percent Malays, 6 percent Indians as well as Arabs, Sri Lankans, Europeans, Indonesians, and Filipinos. "KL," as locals call their city, has developed in the course of a century from a small village into one of the largest and most modern business and commercial cities in South-east Asia.

Kuala Lumpur, 1857 von Zinnminenarbeitern mitten im Urwald gegründet und im Süden der Malaccahalbinsel an den Flüssen Gombak und Kelang gelegen, ist heute Malaysias größte Stadt, Hauptstadt und Kulturmetropole zugleich. Die städtische Bevölkerung setzt sich aus verschiedenen ethnischen Gruppen zusammen: 52 Prozent Chinesen, 39 Prozent Malaien, sechs Prozent Inder sowie Araber, Sri Lanker, Europäer, Indonesier und Philippiner. »KL«, wie die Einheimischen ihre Stadt nennen, entwickelte sich innerhalb von gut einem Jahrhundert von einem kleinen Dorf zu einer der modernsten und größten Geschäfts- und Handelsmetropolen in Südostasien.

Over 44 percent of the gross domestic product of Malaysia is generated by the industries of Kuala Lumpur. The range of products includes electronic goods, wood, and timber products, palm oil, pepper, tin, rubber, as well as mineral oil, and gas. Kuala Lumpur is a pulsating economic center that offers an interesting platform for foreign investors thanks to an attractive legal framework. The growth rate of the gross domestic product in the period 1995–2004 was on average 5.4 percent even though the country's economy suffered enormous losses during the Asian Crisis in 1998. However Kuala Lumpur recovered quickly from this economic recession and is today one of the most rapidly developing cities in Asia.

Über 44 Prozent des Bruttoinlandsprodukts von Malaysia wird von der herstellenden Industrie Kuala Lumpurs entwickelt. Die Produktpalette beinhaltet u.a. elektronische Erzeugnisse, Produkte der Holz- und Forstwirtschaft, Palmöl, Pfeffer, Zinn, Kautschuk sowie Erdöl und Erdgas. Kuala Lumpur bietet als pulsierendes ökonomisches Zentrum aufgrund einer attraktiven Gesetzgebung eine interessante Plattform für ausländische Investoren. Die Wachstumsrate des Bruttoinlandsproduktes lag im Zeitraum 1995–2004 bei durchschnittlich 5,4 Prozent, und das, obwohl die Wirtschaft des Landes zur Zeit der Asienkrise im Jahr 1998 einen enormen Verlust erfuhr. Kuala Lumpur erholte sich jedoch rasch von dieser Wirtschaftskrise und zählt heute zu den sich am schnellsten entwickelten Städte Asiens.

The economic boom, cultural diversity and the combination of many different religions in the city are expressed in Kuala Lumpur's typical urban architecture: alongside high-rise buildings such as the Petronas Towers, the highest twin towers in the world that form a symbol of the rapid economic progress and the development of the banking district, there are remarkable religious buildings such as the Thean Hou Temple, or Masjid Negara, the postmodern national mosque that was completed in 1965, the Cathedral of St. Mary the Virgin, or Sri Mahamariamman the Hindu temple that dates from 1873. These architecturally impressive buildings are evidence of the diversity of cultures and religions that Kuala Lumpur combines with its office and bank buildings.

Wirtschaftlicher Aufschwung, kulturelle Vielfalt und die Vereinigung verschiedenster Religionen in der Stadt äußern sich auch in der für Kuala Lumpur typischen Stadtarchitektur: neben Hochhäusern, z. B. dem Bürogebäude Petronas Towers, den höchsten Zwillingstürmen der Welt, die als Zeichen des rasanten wirtschaftlichen Fortschritts und Aufschwungs das Bankenviertel zieren, finden sich bemerkenswerte Sakralbauten wie der Thean Hou Tempel, die 1965 fertiggestellte postmoderne Nationalmoschee Masjid Negara, die älteste anglikanische Backsteinkirche Cathedral of Virgin St. Mary oder der aus dem Jahr 1873 stammende Hindutempel Sri Mahamariamman. Diese architektonisch beeindruckenden Gebäude legen Zeugnis von der Vielfalt der Kulturen und Religionen ab, die Kuala Lumpur inmitten von Büro- und Bankgebäuden in sich vereint.

MENARA TELEKOM

ARCHITECTS ARCHITEKTEN: **HIJJAS KASTURI ASSOCIATES**
YEAR OF COMPLETION FERTIGSTELLUNG: **2001**
HEIGHT HÖHE: **310 M**

STEEL BAMBOO SHOOT

Its height of 310 meters and its sculptural shape make the Menara Telecom Building, the headquarters of Telecom Malaysia, one of Kuala Lumpur's architectural highlights. The fusion of technology and nature is expressed not only in the organic silhouette, supposedly inspired by the shoots of a bamboo plant, but is made directly tangible in a number of open gardens laid out on different floors of the building. As well as offices and an impressive hall with seating for 2,500, the 55 floors of the building also contain leisure facilities, a daycare center, a fitness center, and medical services for people who work in the building. The helicopter landing pad on the roof is one of the highest in the world.

STÄHLERNER BAMBUSSPROSS

Das Menara Telekom-Gebäude, Hauptsitz der Telekom Malaysia, zählt mit seiner Höhe von 310 Metern und seiner skulpturalen Bauform zu den architektonischen Highlights Kuala Lumpurs. Die Fusion von Technik und Natur kommt nicht nur in der organische Silhouette, die von einer sprießenden Bambuspflanze inspiriert ist, zum Ausdruck, sondern wird geradezu greifbar in mehreren offenen Gärten, die auf verschiedenen Stockwerken angelegt sind. Die 55 Etagen des Baus bieten neben Büroräumen und einem repräsentativen Saal mit 2.500 Plätzen auch einen Freizeitbereich, eine Kindertagesstätte, ein Fitnesszentrum und medizinische Einrichtungen für die Mit-arbeiter. Der Hubschrauberlandeplatz auf dem Dach ist einer der höchsten weltweit.

1 THE FORM OF THE MENARA TELECOM BUILDING RECALLS A BAMBOO PLANT.
DIE FORM DES MENARA TELEKOM-GEBÄUDES ERINNERT AN EINE BAMBUSPFLANZE.
2 THE TOWER IS SPECTACULARLY ILLUMINATED AT NIGHT.
NACHTS IST DER TURM SPEKTAKULÄR BELEUCHTET.
3 THERE IS A HELICOPTER LANDING PAD ON THE ROOF OF THE BUILDING.
AUF DEM DACH DES GEBÄUDES BEFINDET SICH EIN HUB-SCHRAUBERLANDEPLATZ.
4 AN INNOVATIVE LIGHTING CONCEPT LENDS THE INTERIORS AN EXTRAVAGANT ATMOSPHERE.
EIN INNOVATIVES BELEUCHTUNGSKONZEPT VERLEIHT DEN INNENRÄUMEN EINE EXTRAVAGANTE ATMOSPHÄRE.

PETRONAS TOWERS

ARCHITECTS ARCHITEKTEN: **CESAR PELLI & ASSOCIATES**

YEAR OF COMPLETION FERTIGSTELLUNG: **1998**

AREA FLÄCHE: **697,000 M²**

1 THE 452-METER-HIGH PETRONAS TWIN TOWERS OCCUPY THE 100-ACRE SITE OF A FORMER
RACETRACK AND HAVE BECOME THE CITY'S LANDMARK.
DIE 452 METER HOHEN PETRONAS TWIN TOWERS STEHEN AUF DEM ETWA 40 HEKTAR GROSSEN
GELÄNDE EINER EHEMALIGEN RENNSTRECKE UND WURDEN ZUM WAHRZEICHEN DER STADT.
2 THE BUILDING'S FACADE WAS STRONGLY INSPIRED BY ISLAMIC FORMS.
DIE FASSADE DES GEBÄUDES WURDE STARK VON ISLAMISCHEN FORMEN BEEINFLUSST.
3 THE SKYBRIDGE ON THE 41ST AND 42ND FLOORS IS ALMOST 60 METERS LONG AND CONNECTS
THE TWO TOWERS.
DIE BEINAHE 60 METER LANGE »SKYBRIDGE« VERBINDET DIE BEIDEN TÜRME ZWISCHEN DEM
41. UND 42. STOCKWERK.

TWIN ELEGANCE

The highest building in the world before being overtaken by Taipei 101,
the Petronas Twin Towers were built for a variety of commercial and
public uses by Malaysia's state petroleum company. Designed by Cesar
Pelli—responsible for the World Financial Center in New York City—
the architect's idea was that the towers symbolize a large gateway to
Kuala Lumpur in a western-style complex. Partly inspired by geometric
Islamic patterns in the form of two intersecting squares which create
an eight-point star, the walls of each point curve outwards furthering
the towers' arabesque appearance. The skybridge, which links the
two structures at 160 meters between the 41st and 42nd floors, was
constructed so that it was able to move independently of the two buildings. The facade consists of polished steel elements and glass, which
reflect light from the surrounding area. The building is also fitted with
an intricate, award-winning lighting system that gives it its brilliant
night-time appearance.

DOPPELTE ELEGANZ

Die Zwillingstürme waren das höchste Gebäude der Welt, bis sie vom
Taipei 101 überholt wurden. Die von der staatlichen Mineralölgesellschaft
erbauten Petronas Towers beherbergen eine ganze Reihe von gewerb-
lichen und öffentlichen Nutzungen. Die Entwurfsidee von Cesar Pelli,
der auch das World Financial Center in New York City baute, sieht die
Türme als symbolisches überdimensionales Tor zu Kuala Lumpur,
integriert in einen Komplex im westlichen Stil. Die Form des Gebäudes
wurde teilweise von islamischen Mustern beeinflusst, sie besteht aus
zwei sich überlagernden Quadraten, die einen achteckigen Stern bilden.
An den Schnittstellen wurden die Wände halbkreisförmig ausgeführt,
was die arabeske Anmutung des Turms noch verstärkt. Die »Skybridge«,
die die beiden Gebäude zwischen dem 41. und 42. Stock in einer Höhe
von 160 Metern verbindet, wurde so konstruiert, dass sie von den unterschiedlichen Eigenbewegungen der Türme unabhängig ist. Die Fassade
besteht aus polierten Edelstahlelementen und Glas, die das Licht der
Umgebung spiegeln. Außerdem verfügt das Gebäude über ein aufwen-
diges, ausgezeichnetes Beleuchtungssystem, das ihm auch bei Nacht
einen brillanten Auftritt verschafft.

LIVING IN STYLE

Overlooking Kuala Lumpur's iconic Petronas Towers, the Troika development by Foster and Partners will be Malaysia's tallest residential complex when completed in 2009. Located in the Kuala Lumpur City Center Park, the three towers will have 38, 44, and 50 floors respectively. With the twisted shape of the buildings, all apartments have the best possible views over the capital. 172 in total, they differ in size from 200 to 300 square meters, and penthouses of 500 square meters. Similar to the Petronas Towers skybridges link the three buildings on the 24th level which features a pool and a common reception area. The easily accessible roofs are designed in such a way that recreational activity can take place on them. The towers are situated in a mixed development area that will also accommodate boutiques, offices, retail outlets, and restaurants. A motor-free courtyard will provide tranquility in the heart of the city.

STILVOLL LEBEN

Das Bauprojekt Troika von Foster and Partners wird nach seiner Fertigstellung 2009 der größte Wohnkomplex Malaysias sein. Die drei im Kuala Lumpur City Center Park gelegenen Türme mit Ausblick auf Kuala Lumpurs Wahrzeichen, die Petronas Towers, werden 38, 44 und 50 Stockwerke hoch sein. Die gedrehte Form des Gebäudes sorgt dafür, dass alle Wohnungen den bestmöglichen Blick über die Stadt bieten. Insgesamt sollen 172 Wohnungen mit 200 bis 300 Quadratmetern Wohnfläche entstehen, die Penthouses verfügen über 500 Quadratmeter. Ähnlich wie die Petronas Towers werden die Gebäude im 24. Stockwerk über »Skybridges« verbunden, hier befinden sich ein Schwimmbad und der Empfangsbereich. Die gut zugänglichen Dächer sind für Freizeitaktivitäten vorgesehen. Die Türme liegen in einem Gebiet mit gemischter Nutzung, in dem sich auch Boutiquen, Büros, Einzelhandelsgeschäfte und Restaurants befinden. Ein autofreier Innenhof wird mitten im Herzen der Stadt Ruhe bringen.

1 THREE RESIDENTIAL SHEAR-WALLED BUILDINGS OF VARYING HEIGHT MAKE UP THE TROIKA DEVELOPMENT.
DAS TROIKA-PROJEKT BESTEHT AUS DREI AUS WANDSCHEIBEN AUFGEBAUTEN WOHNTÜRMEN IN UNTERSCHIEDLICHEN HÖHEN.
2 THE SPECTACULAR VIEWS FROM THE SKYBRIDGE ONTO KULA LUMPUR'S SKYLINE.
DER SPEKTAKULÄRE BLICK VON DER »SKYBRIDGE« AUF DIE SKYLINE VON KUALA LUMPUR.
3 THE CLEAR MODERN FORM OF THE TROIKA DISTINGUISHES IT FROM THE MORE MALAYSIAN-STYLE PETRONAS TWIN TOWERS IN THE BACKGROUND.
TROIKA UNTERSCHEIDET SICH DURCH SEINE KLARE MODERNE FORM VON DEN PETRONAS TOWERS IM HINTERGRUND, DIE EHER IM MALAYSISCHEN STIL GEHALTEN SIND.

THE TROIKA

ARCHITECTS ARCHITEKTEN: **FOSTER AND PARTNERS**
YEAR OF COMPLETION FERTIGSTELLUNG: **2009**

SEOUL

SEOUL

POPULATION EINWOHNERZAHL: 10,700,000 IN THE METROPOLITAN AREA
IN DER METROPOLREGION; 21,700,000 INCLUDING THE CITIES OF INCHEON, SUWON, GOYANG, AND
SEONGNAM EINSCHLIESSLICH DER MILLIONENSTÄDTE INCHEON, SUWON, GOYANG UND SEONGNAM
POPULATION DENSITY EINWOHNERDICHTE: 17,092 PERSONS PER KM²
AREA FLÄCHE: 605 KM²
WEBSITE: HTTP://ENGLISH.SEOUL.GO.KR

Around forty-three percent of the population of South Korea is concentrated in Seoul, which has been the capital of South Korea since the partition of the country in 1948, and in the neighboring satellite towns—on only 0.6 percent of the total area of the country. Therefore Seoul has a population density of 17,092 inhabitants per square kilometer. The urban population is extremely homogeneous: the proportion of foreigners is only 1.3 percent: the largest groups are the Chinese (ca. 77,000), the Americans (ca. 11,000) and the Japanese (ca. 6,700). After Tokyo and Mexico City Seoul and its metropolitan region is the third largest city in the world. It is divided into 25 urban districts, known as *gu* that are subdivided into numerous smaller (522 *dong*, 13,787 *tong* and 102,796 *ban* districts).

In Seoul – seit der Teilung des Landes im Jahr 1948 die Hauptstadt Südkoreas – und den angrenzenden Satellitenstädten konzentrieren sich auf 0,6 Prozent der Landesfläche rund 43 Prozent aller Südkoreaner. Damit hat Seoul eine Bevölkerungsdichte, die 17.092 Einwohner pro Quadratkilometer beträgt. Die Stadtbevölkerung ist sehr homogen, der Anteil ausländischer Bewohner liegt bei lediglich 1,3 Prozent: Die größten ausländischen Bevölkerungsgruppen sind Chinesen (ca. 77.000), Amerikaner (ca. 11.000) und Japaner (ca. 6.700). Nach Tokio und Mexiko-Stadt ist Seoul mit seiner Metropolregion die drittgrößte Stadt weltweit. Die Stadt gliedert sich in 25 Stadtbezirke, *gu* genannt, die wiederum in unzählige Unterbezirke (522 *dong*-, 13.787 *tong*- und 102,796 *ban*-Bezirke) unterteilt sind.

Rapid transformation into an industrial society following the Korean War meant that South Korea with its enormous economic growth and a gross domestic product of 786 billion US dollars advanced within a short period to the tenth most important trading nation in the world. After the Asian Crisis in 1997 that also affected South Korea the government placed increased emphasis on internationalization and globalization. The country's membership of the World Trade Organization (WTO) and of the OECD in 1996, as well as the measures employed to overcome the Asian economic crisis led to renewed efforts to liberalize and deregulate the economy and made Seoul into one of the most interesting markets and investment locations for foreign companies. Seventy percent of South Korean economic growth is generated by exports. This figure represents about two-fifths of the gross domestic product.

Der rasante Wandel zur industriellen Gesellschaft nach dem Koreakrieg bewirkte, dass Südkorea aufgrund seines immensen Wirtschaftswachstums mit einem Bruttoinlandsprodukt von 786 Milliarden US-Dollar binnen kurzer Zeit zur zehntgrößten Handelsnation der Welt avancierte. Nach der asiatischen Finanzkrise, die 1997 auch Südkorea erfasste, setzte die Regierung verstärkt auf Internationalisierung und Globalisierung. Der Beitritt zur Welthandelsorganisation (WTO) und zur OECD im Jahr 1996, aber auch die Maßnahmen zur Überwindung der asiatischen Wirtschaftskrise führten zu einer Verstärkung von Liberalisierungs- und Deregulierungsmaßnahmen, wodurch Seoul zu einem höchst interessanten Absatzmarkt und Investitionsstandort für ausländische Unternehmen wurde. 70 Prozent des südkoreanischen Wirtschaftswachstums wird durch den Export generiert. Das entspricht in etwa zwei Fünfteln des Bruttoinlandsprodukts.

After the end of the Korean War in 1953 the military government drew up a plan for the rapid reconstruction of Seoul that did not envisage the use of traditional building methods. Hence most buildings in Seoul—with the exception of palaces, temples, cemeteries, and fortresses—date from the 1960s and later. Numerous skyscrapers and multi-storey apartment buildings for families were erected around this time, as living accommodation had to be provided for the rapidly growing population (the three million barrier was broken in 1963). The government also undertook efforts to restrict population growth in the urban area itself. Today Seoul combines the past with modernity: In the small side streets the contrast between high-rise buildings and historical structures helps form the architectural impression made by the city.

Nach dem Ende des Koreakriegs im Jahr 1953 wurde von der Militärregierung ein Plan für den zügigen Wiederaufbau Seouls entworfen, in dem traditionelle Bauweisen nicht vorgesehen waren. Die meisten Gebäude in Seoul – mit Ausnahme von Palästen, Tempeln, Gräbern und Wehranlangen – stammen aus den 1960er Jahren und später. Zahlreiche Wolkenkratzer und mehrstöckige Apartmenthäuser für Familien entstanden zu dieser Zeit, da für die in den Nachkriegsjahren wieder rasch ansteigende Bevölkerungszahl (1963 wurde die 3-Millionen-Grenze überschritten) Platz geschaffen werden musste. Die Regierung bemühte sich darüber hinaus, die Bevölkerung in den Satellitenstädten anzusiedeln, um dem Bevölkerungswachstum im eigentlichen Stadtgebiet entgegenzuwirken. Das Stadtbild änderte sich massiv. Heute vereint Seoul die Vergangenheit mit der Moderne: In den kleinen Gassen zeichnet das Wechselspiel zwischen Hochhäusern und historischen Gebäuden das architektonische Bild der Stadt.

1 THE CUBIC FORMS OF THE BOUTIQUE MONACO BUILDING ARE
DESIGNED TO HARMONIZE WITH THE BUILT SURROUNDINGS.
DIE KUBISCHEN FORMEN DES BOUTIQUE MONACO-GEBAUDES
SIND DER BAULICHEN UMGEBUNG ANGEGLICHEN.
2 THIS RESIDENTIAL AND COMMERCIAL BUILDING CONSISTS
OF 172 DIFFERENT UNITS LINKED TO EACH OTHER.
DAS WOHN- UND GESCHAFTSHAUS BESTEHT AUS 172 MIT-
EINANDER VERBUNDENEN BAUEINHEITEN.
3 LUXURIANT VEGETATION AT THE BASE OF THE BUILDING AS
WELL AS AT THE ELEVATED OUTDOOR AREAS PROVIDES PLACES
FOR RECREATION.
UPPIGE BEPFLANZUNG AN DER BASIS DES BAUS SOWIE AN
DEN HÖHER GELEGENEN AUSSENFLÄCHEN SCHAFFEN ORTE
DER ERHOLUNG.
4 A NUMBER OF OUTDOOR AREAS ARE DISTRIBUTED THROUGH-
OUT THE BUILDING.
MEHRERE AUSSENFLÄCHEN SIND ÜBER DEN BAU VERTEILT.

MODERN LIVING

Boutique Monaco, a commercial and residential building designed
by Minsuk Cho, looks something like an oversized puzzle. This tower
is being erected in the heart of Seoul, close to Gangnam Station, and
consists of 172 building units that are connected to each other and
offer 49 different variations in terms of layout and design The different
possible functions extend from an exclusive apartment to a modern
office or to units fitted out as a restaurant, shop, cultural facility, or
fitness centre. The building will have "vertical" outdoor areas at certain
points that can be accessed from several different floors. These external areas are distributed throughout the complex in such a way that
from each of the building's 27 floors it will be possible to reach an
outdoor space.

MODERNES WOHNEN

Wie ein überdimensionales Puzzle präsentiert sich das von Minsuk
Cho entworfene Geschäfts- und Wohngebäude Boutique Monaco. Der
Turm im Herzen Seouls, der nahe der Gangnam Station errichtet wird,
besteht aus 172 miteinander verbundenen Baueinheiten, die in Bezug
auf Grundriss und Gestaltung 49 verschiedene Varianten aufweisen.
Ihre Nutzungsmöglichkeiten reichen von edlem Appartement über
modernes Büro bis hin zur Ausstattung als Restaurant, Geschäft, Kul-
tureinrichtung oder Fitnesszentrum. Der Baukörper wird an einigen
Stellen »vertikale« Außenflächen aufweisen, die von mehreren Stockwerken gleichzeitig zugänglich sind. Diese Außenflächen sind so über
das Gebäude verteilt, dass von jeder der 27 Etagen aus ein Freiluft-
bereich zugänglich sein wird.

BOUTIQUE MONACO

ARCHITECTS ARCHITEKTEN: **MINSUK CHO MASS STUDIES**
YEAR OF COMPLETION FERTIGSTELLUNG: **2008**
AREA FLÄCHE: **54,500 M²**

1 OVERALL VIEW OF THE DONGBU FINANCE CENTER, 891-10, DAECHI-DONG, GANGNAM-GU, SEOUL.
GESAMTANSICHT DES DONGBU FINANCE CENTER, 891-10, DAECHI-DONG, GANGNAM-GU, SEOUL.
2 THE ILLUMINATION OF THE FLOORS EMPHASIZES THE HORIZONTAL ARTICULATION MORE STRONGLY THAN THE VERTICAL.
DURCH DIE STOCKWERKSBELEUCHTUNG TRITT DIE HORIZONTALE GLIEDERUNG GEGENÜBER DER VERTIKALEN STÄRKER HERVOR.
3 NIGHT TIME ILLUMINATION OF AREAS OF GLAZING PLACED BESIDE EACH OTHER AT THE BASE OF THE BUILDING.
NÄCHTLICHE BELEUCHTUNG DER NEBENEINANDER GESETZTEN GLASFLÄCHEN DES SOCKELBEREICHES.
4 A DETAIL OF THE HORIZONTAL ARTICULATION OF THE NORTH SIDE, SEEN IN THE SUNLIGHT.
EIN DETAIL DER NORDSEITIGEN HORIZONTALGLIEDERUNG IM SONNENLICHT.

PATCHWORK

Even from a considerable distance the 152.25-metre-high Dongbu Finance Center in the Gangnam district of southeastern Seoul attracts one's attention—less on account of its height and more because of its sculptural form that reaches into urban space. While the west, south and east-facing sides of this glass and steel building are even and vertical, the northern side, which is the principal facade of the building to the main street, looks as if layers of a homogeneous building fabric have been applied in different shapes and thicknesses to create an almost organic building. This patchwork technique in which differently colored and shaped areas of glazing are placed on each other has also been employed in the base of the building. The variety of fields in which the client—the Seoul Dongbu concern—operates, as well as the traditional Korean technique of *shik-tak-bo* (layering and combining material), have here been brought together in a homogeneous urban synthesis that impressively combines local tradition with global modernity.

PATCHWORK

Schon von weitem fällt das 152,25 Meter hohe Dongbu Finance Center im Bezirk Gangnam im südöstlichen Seoul ins Auge – weniger durch seine bloße Höhe, als vielmehr durch seine skulpturale, in den Raum drängende Form. Sind die nach Westen, Süden und Osten weisenden Flächen der Glas- und Stahlarchitektur plan und lotrecht, wirkt die Nordfläche, die Schauseite des Gebäudes zur Hauptstraße hin, als wären verschiedene Schichten gleichartiger Bausubstanz in unterschiedlichem Zuschnitt und Dicke zu einem fast organisch anmutenden Baukörper aufgetragen worden. Auch am Sockel des Gebäudes findet sich diese patchworkartige Technik, in der verschiedenfarbige und unterschiedlich geformte Glasflächen aneinandergesetzt werden. Die Vielseitigkeit der Geschäftsfelder des auftraggebenden Seouler Konzerns Dongbu, wie auch die traditionelle koreanische Technik des *shik-tak-bo*, des (Stoffe) an- und Übereinanderschichtens, haben hier eine homogene, urbane Synthese gefunden, die lokale Tradition und globale Modernität eindrucksvoll vereint.

DONGBU FINANCE CENTER

ARCHITECTS ARCHITEKTEN: **KOHN PEDERSEN FOX ASSOCIATES**
YEAR OF COMPLETION FERTIGSTELLUNG: **2002**
AREA FLÄCHE: **1,288.09 M²**

TRANSPORTATION CENTER
INCHON INTERNATIONAL AIRPORT

ARCHITECTS ARCHITEKTEN: **TERRY FARRELL & PARTNERS**
YEAR OF COMPLETION FERTIGSTELLUNG: **2002**
AREA FLÄCHE: **250,000 M²**

THE CRANE

Like Hong Kong's Chep Lap Kok airport, Inchon International was built on reclaimed land about 45 minutes west of Seoul. Probably the most technologically advanced airport in Asia it has a service capacity of around 50 million passengers per annum and is currently Asia's seventh busiest airport. The airport's biomorphically-shaped Transportation Center, built by British architects Terry Farrell & Partners, contains stations for three rail networks (metro, standard, and high-speed) as well as an advanced circulation system of escalators, elevators, stairs, and ramps, most of which are underground. The so-called Great Hall, with its aerofoil roof of stainless steel panels and glass, has a big central concourse through which all passengers pass when arriving and departing from the airport. A steel portal truss structure evoking the movement of a bird, vaults over the hall which, along with its pod-like flight control center, give the overall structure an extremely dynamic, futuristic feel.

DER KRANICH

Der Inchon International Airport wurde genau wie der Flughafen Chep Lap Kok in Hongkong auf künstlich aufgeschüttetem Land gebaut und liegt etwa 45 Minuten westlich von Seoul. Der technologisch wohl fortschrittlichste Flughafen Asiens verfügt über eine Kapazität von etwa 50 Millionen Passagieren pro Jahr und liegt damit bei den verkehrsreichsten Flughäfen in Asien an siebter Stelle. In dem biomorph geformten Transportation Center, das von den britischen Architekten Terry Farrell & Partners gebaut wurde, sind die Bahnhöfe für drei Bahnnetze untergebracht, außerdem ein ausgeklügeltes Verbindungssystem aus meist unterirdischen Rolltreppen, Aufzügen, Treppen und Rampen. In der sogenannten Great Hall liegt unter einem Dach aus Edelstahlplatten und Glas in Form eines Tragflügels die große zentrale Wartehalle, die alle ankommenden und abfliegenden Passagiere durchqueren. Die Stahlträgerkonstruktion, die die Halle überspannt, erinnert an einen fliegenden Vogel und sorgt zusammen mit dem gondelförmigen Flugkontrollzentrum für eine dynamische und futuristische Anmutung.

SHANGHAI

SHANGHAI

POPULATION EINWOHNERZAHL: CA. 9,838,000 CITY STADTZENTRUM;
17,420,000 GREATER METROPOLITAN AREA METROPOLREGION
POPULATION DENSITY EINWOHNERDICHTE: 2,750 PERSONS PER KM² (GREATER METROPOLITAN METROPOLREGION)
AREA FLÄCHE: 550 KM² (CITY STADTZENTRUM); 6.340,5 KM² (GREATER METROPOLITAN AREA METROPOLREGION)
WEBSITE: WWW.SHANGHAI.GOV.CN

Shanghai, situated on the delta of the Jangtse River, is China's largest city with a population of over seventeen million. Along with the city's liberalization and economic boom, the "Paris of the East" has also experienced a strong increase in population mainly due to increased migration from the surrounding rural areas. Within the city limits alone and despite the strict registration systems, the number of inhabitants has grown by three million since the early 1980s; an even greater growth rate is evident in the extended metropolitan areas.

Shanghai, am Delta des Jangtse-Flusses gelegen, gilt mit über 17 Millionen Einwohnern in der Metropolregion als größte Stadt Chinas. Das »Paris des Ostens« erlebte mit der Liberalisierung der Wirtschaft ein starkes Bevölkerungswachstum, das zum großen Teil dem Zuzug der Landbevölkerung zuzuschreiben ist: Allein im eigentlichen Stadtgebiet erhöhte sich die Einwohnerzahl trotz des strengen Melde- und Registrierungssystems seit den frühen 1980er Jahren um drei Millionen, an den Randgebieten der Metropole ist ebenfalls starker Zuwachs festzustellen.

Nowhere else in China has a city's rise to a major economic player been so tangible as in Shanghai. The metropolis has even surpassed Shenzhen and Guangzhou who first profited from the Chinese business reform at the end of the 1970s. Since the early 1990s, Shanghai's economic growth can be measured in double digits. After Hong Kong and Singapore, Shanghai's harbor has the highest turnover in money and goods worldwide. The growing prosperity of Shanghai's upper echelon along with the constant increase in tourism has encouraged individual expenditure. Shopping streets like Nanjing Lu and Huaihai Lu are aglow in the brilliance of new and choice department stores.

Nirgends wird Chinas Entwicklung zum ökonomischen Riesen spürbarer als in Shanghai. Nachdem zuerst Shenzhen und Guangzhou von den chinesischen Wirtschaftsreformen Ende der 1970er Jahre profitierten, hat Shanghai die beiden Städte mittlerweile überholt. Seit Anfang der 1990er Jahre liegt das hiesige Wirtschaftswachstum im zweistelligen Bereich. Nach Hongkong und Singapur hat Shanghai den größten und umschlagstärksten Hafen der Welt. Der steigende Wohlstand der Shanghaier Oberschicht sowie zunehmender Tourismus fördern den privaten Konsum, Shoppingmeilen wie die Nanjing Lu oder die Huaihai Lu erstrahlen im Glanz neuer Nobelkaufhäuser.

Shanghai's architecture embodies China's economic boom more than
any other city. The skyline of the new financial district, Pudong, is
a constructed vision of the future in a constant state of flux. Over
6,000 skyscrapers make evident the intense construction boom that
has marked Shanghai over in recent years and that is not tapering off.
The large demand for centrally located living and working space has
forced the market to build upwards with the prices for property steadily increasing. Besides quantity, the aesthetic value of the individual projects
is becoming increasingly important with the design and realization of
ever more prestigious projects being allocated to domestic and foreign
firms. The downside of this massive increase in building activity, and
the need to find space for new buildings, has been the destruction of
the traditional architectural fabric of the city, much of which is from
the early twentieth century.

Shanghai verkörpert auch architektonisch den wirtschaftlichen Aufschwung Chinas wie keine andere Stadt: Die Skyline des neuen Finanz-
distrikts Pudong ist ein gebauter Blick in die Zukunft, im ständigen
Wandel begriffen. Mehr als 6.000 Hochhäuser bezeugen den beispiel-
losen Bauboom, der Shanghai in den letzten Jahren prägte und der immer
noch anhält. Die große Nachfrage nach zentralen Wohn- und Geschäfts-
räumen forciert den Trend in die Höhe, gleichzeitig steigen die Preise
für Immobilien stark an. Neben Quantität zählt gerade für Prestige-
projekte auch ästhetische Qualität, Aufträge für neue Büro- und Ladenbauten werden vermehrt an renommierte Architekturbüros aus dem
In- und Ausland vergeben. Die Schattenseite der regen Bautätigkeit ist
der Verlust von alter Substanz: Um Platz für Neubauten zu schaffen,
werden viele traditionelle Wohnviertel aus dem frühen 20. Jahrhundert
abgerissen.

BUND CENTER

ARCHITECTS ARCHITEKTEN: **JOHN PORTMANN AND ASSOCIATES**
YEAR OF COMPLETION FERTIGSTELLUNG: **2002**
AREA FLÄCHE: **20,000 M²**
HEIGHT HÖHE: **45 FLOORS** STOCKWERKE

1 THE THREE TOWERED BUND CENTER ACCOMMODATES THE WESTIN SHANGHAI HOTEL AND IS THE HEAD OFFICES FOR A NUMBER OF MULTINATIONAL CORPORATIONS.
DIE DREI TÜRME DES BUND CENTER SIND SITZ DES WESTIN SHANGHAI HOTELS SOWIE EINIGER INTERNATIONALER UNTERNEHMEN.
2 THE SIMPLE BRICK AND GLASS EXTERIOR WAS DESIGNED TO SUIT THE VARIED URBAN CONTEXT.
DAS SCHLICHTE GEBÄUDEÄUSSERE AUS STEIN UND GLAS FÜGT SICH IN DIE BAULICHE UMGEBUNG EIN.
3 A SCULPTURE GARDEN ADORNS THE INTERIOR WITH A CAFE AND SCREEN IN THE BACKGROUND.
IM INNEREN IST EIN SKULPTURENGARTEN ANGELEGT, DANEBEN BEFINDET SICH EIN CAFÉ.
4 SEEN FROM PUDONG, THE BUILDING'S LOTUS-INSPIRED CROWN ILLUMINATES THE NIGHT SKY.
BLICK VON PUDONG AUF DEN BUND: DIE LOTUSBLÜTENFÖRMIGE KRONE DES BAUS LEUCHTET IN DER NACHT.

SHANGHAI'S CROWN

Located in the Bund's historic financial district, this three tower, mixed-use project houses the Westin Shanghai hotel along with functioning as a corporate address for a number of companies including Hewlett Packard, Microsoft, and Toshiba. The hotel with its 303 guest rooms, spa, restaurant, entertainment, and conference facilities has become a major meeting point for Shanghai's business community. At night its glowing crown—582.5 tons heavy and eleven meters tall—forms a striking focal point on Shanghai's skyline. The crown's ring is intended to signify eternity while the two concentric layers of draping lotus leaf petals imply growth and prosperity. The otherwise simple symmetrical form with a facade mostly made up of stone and glass, was developed to fit into its surrounding context.

SHANGHAIS KRONE

Dieser Komplex mit seinen drei Türmen liegt im historischen Finanzdistrikt des Bund-Viertels und beherbergt neben dem Westin Shanghai Hotel einige Firmenniederlassungen, darunter Hewlett Packard, Microsoft und Toshiba. Mit seinen 303 Gästezimmern, einem Spa, einem Restaurant und Konferenz- sowie Veranstaltungsräumen gilt das Hotel als wichtige Tagungsstätte für geschäftliche Termine. Die »Krone« des Bund Center, die eine Höhe von elf Metern aufweist und 582,5 Tonnen wiegt, gehört zu den markanten Punkten der Skyline Shanghais – besonders nachts, im beleuchteten Zustand. Während die Ringform des Gebäudeabschlusses Unendlichkeit symbolisiert, stehen die zweilagigen Lotusblütenblätter für Wachstum und Wohlstand. Die ansonsten schlichte symmetrische Form des Baus mit seiner Fassade aus Glas und Stein gliedert sich architektonisch in die Umgebung ein.

JIN MAO TOWER

ARCHITECTS ARCHITEKTEN: **SOM**
(SKIDMORE, OWINGS & MERRILL)
YEAR OF COMPLETION FERTIGSTELLUNG: **1998**
AREA FLÄCHE: **278,707 M²**
HEIGHT HÖHE: **88 FLOORS** STOCKWERKE

SHANGHAI'S MAIN MARKER

Housing the city's Hyatt Hotel on 34 floors with 555 rooms as well as bars, cafés, restaurants, health spas, and even a swimming pool, this dominant marker on Shanghai's skyline is currently the tallest building in China with its 88 floors (the top floor is 366 meters high). The staggered construction was developed with references to the number eight, associated with prosperity in China, and is built around an octogan-shaped concrete shear wall core with eight exterior composite super-columns and eight steel columns. The foundations are almost 100 meters deep to counteract the poor soil conditions in the area and can withstand winds up to 200 km / h, as well as earthquakes with the force of 7 on the Richter scale. Sixty-one elevators and nineteen escalators carry visitors through the building with the indoor observation deck on the top floor offering spectacular panoramic views across the whole of Shanghai.

DAS WAHRZEICHEN SHANGHAIS

Dieses die Skyline Shanghais dominierende Hochhaus ist mit insgesamt 88 Stockwerken derzeit das höchste Gebäude Chinas (die oberste Etage liegt bei 366 Metern). Auf 34 Geschossen logiert das Hyatt Hotel, das neben 555 Zimmern auch Bars, Cafés, Restaurants, Spas und sogar einen Swimming Pool zu bieten hat. Die Struktur des Baus mit seiner stufige Fassade birgt Referenzen an die Zahl acht, die in China als Glückszahl gilt: Der statische Kern in der Mitte ist achteckig, ebenso die Außenhülle. Der Turm ruht auf Stahlfundamenten, die fast 100 Meter in die Tiefe reichen. Diese sichern die Standfestigkeit des Baus bei Windstärken bis zu 200 km / h oder Erdbeben bis zur Stärke 7 auf der Richterskala. Den Besuchern stehen 61 Aufzüge und 19 Rolltreppen zur Verfügung, und ein Aussichtsdeck im obersten Stockwerk ermöglicht einen spektakulären Panoramablick auf Shanghai.

1 IN ITS FORM, JIN MAO TOWER IS BASED ON THE MODEL OF CHINESE PAGODAS
DER TURM GREIFT IN SEINER FORM AUF CHINESISCHE PAGODEN ZURÜCK.
2 THE OBSERVATION DECK ON THE 88TH FLOOR.
DIE AUSSICHTSPLATTFORM IM 88. STOCK.
3 DETAIL SHOWING THE STRUCTURE OF THE FACADE.
AUSSCHNITT DER FASSADE.
4 VIEW UPWARD FROM THE HYATT HOTEL'S ATRIUM ON THE 53RD FLOOR.
BLICK VOM ATRIUM DES HYATT HOTELS IM 53. GESCHOSS NACH OBEN.

MUSEUM OF SCIENCE
AND TECHOLOGY

ARCHITECTS ARCHITEKTEN: **RTKL ASSOCIATES**
YEAR OF COMPLETION FERTIGSTELLUNG: **2001**
AREA FLÄCHE: **89,000 M²**

MONUMENT OF PROGRESS

Shanghai's Museum of Science and Technology is a high-tech prestige project built in the commercial sector Pudong. The sense of progress is made evident in the architecture: the ascending construction of the building symbolizes the rapid development of the city. The optical centerpiece of the structure is a glass sphere that breaks through the roof—in reality an ellipsoid—located in the entrance hall of the museum. This architectural element carries multiple associations from a nucleus to an egg cell to a planet. With its large variety of specially themed areas, showcased in large exhibition halls, the museum has quickly become an major attraction for visitors to Shanghai.

MONUMENT DES FORTSCHRITTS

Shanghais Wissenschafts- und Technikmuseum ist ein High-Tech-Prestigeprojekt, errichtet im Geschäftsviertel Pudong. Das Thema des Fortschritts ist auch in der Architektur präsent, so versinnbildlicht die aufstrebende Struktur des Gebäudes die rasante Entwicklung der Stadt. Optischer Mittelpunkt des Baus ist eine das Dach durchbrechende gläserne Kugel – eigentlich ein Ellipsoid – im Eingangsbereich des Museums. Dieses architektonische Element lässt verschiedene Assoziationen zu, vom Nukleus über die Eizelle bis hin zum Planeten. Mit seinen vielen thematisch spezifizierten Bereichen, präsentiert in großzügigen Ausstellungshallen, hat sich das Museum in kürzester Zeit zum Besuchermagneten entwickelt.

1 THROUGH THE GLASS FACADE THE DIVISION BETWEEN THE INTERIOR AND EXTERIOR DISOLVES.
DIE GLÄSERNE FASSADE DES MUSEUMS LÄSST DIE GRENZEN ZWISCHEN INNEN UND AUSSEN VERSCHWIMMEN.
2 THE TRANSPARENT SPHERE IS BOTH THE CENTERPRIECE AND THE ENTRANCE HALL OF THE BUILDING.
DIE TRANSPARENTE KUGELFORM IST MITTELPUNKT UND EINGANGSBEREICH DES GEBÄUDES.
3 THE OPEN STRUCTURE AND EXPANSIVE EXHIBITION HALLS INVITE VISITORS TO LINGER.
DIE OFFENEN STRUKTUREN UND WEITLÄUFIGEN AUSSTELLUNGSBEREICHE LADEN ZUM VERWEILEN EIN.
4 THE UPWARD SLANTING ROOF SYMBOLIZES VITALITY AND PROGRESS.
DAS AUFSTEIGENDE DACH SYMBOLISIERT DYNAMIK UND FORTSCHRITT.

SPARKLING JEWEL

Paul Andreu's Oriental Art Center is the home of the Shanghai Philharmonic Orchestra and the first concert hall in the city. This building, its shape remenicent of the blossom of a butterfly orchid, has a transparent facade made of over 4,000 individual glass pannels. The vertical tracks of climbing ceramic tiles in the auditorium's lobby areas give the interior an inimitable atmosphere. Besides two large concert halls holding just under 2,000 and 1,100 seats respectively, the Oriental Art Center also has a room with 300 seats for more intimate performances. The Center was constructed using the most recent technology: its acustics are optimal for musical performances of all kinds.

FUNKELNDES JUWEL

Paul Andreus Oriental Art Center ist das Stammhaus des Philharmonischen Orchesters Shanghai und die erste Konzerthalle der Stadt. Das Gebäude, dessen Form an die Blüte einer Schmetterlingsorchidee erinnert, hat eine transparente Fassade aus über 4.000 einzelnen Glasscheiben. Im Inneren verleihen in vertikalen Bahnen verlaufende Keramikfliesen den Bereichen vor den Veranstaltungsräumen eine besondere Note. Neben zwei großen Sälen mit knapp 2.000 beziehungsweise 1.100 Plätzen bietet das Oriental Art Center auch einen Raum mit 300 Plätzen für Aufführungen im kleineren Rahmen. Das Haus wurde mit modernster Technik ausgestattet, die Akustik ist für alle Arten der musikalischen Darbietung optimiert.

1 IN THE EVENINGS THE ORIENTAL ART CENTER TRANSFORMS ITSELF INTO A SPARKLING JEWEL. THE LIGHTS AND COLORS CHANGE ACCORDING TO THE TYPE OF PERFORMANCE.
NACHTS VERWANDELT SICH DAS ORIENTAL ART CENTER IN EIN LEUCHTENDES JUWEL. DIE LICHTER UND FARBEN WECHSELN JE NACH ART DER AUFFÜHRUNG.
2 110,000 TILES FROM YIXING COVER THE WALLS OF THE BUILDING'S INTERIOR.
110.000 FLIESEN AUS DER CHINESISCHEN STADT YIXING VERKLEIDEN DIE WÄNDE DES GEBÄUDEINNEREN.
3 THE CONCERT HALLS HAVE ALL BEEN FITTED WITH THE MOST UP-TO-DATE TECHNOLOGY.
DIE KONZERTSÄLE SIND MIT MODERNSTER TECHNIK AUSGESTATTET.
4 THE BUILDING'S FORM WAS INSPIRED BY THE BLOSSOM OF A BUTTERFLY ORCHID.
DIE FORM DES BAUS IST VON DER BLÜTE DER SCHMETTERLINGSORCHIDEE INSPIRIERT.

ORIENTAL ART CENTER

ARCHITECT ARCHITEKT: **PAUL ANDREU ARCHITECTE WITH ADPI AND ECADI**
AREA FLÄCHE: **39,694 M²**
YEAR OF COMPLETION FERTIGSTELLUNG: **2004**

QI ZHONG INTERNATIONAL TENNIS CENTER

ARCHITECTS ARCHITEKTEN: **MITSURU SENDA AND EDI (ENVIRONMENT DESIGN INSTITUTE)**

YEAR OF COMPLETION FERTIGSTELLUNG: **2005**

AREA FLÄCHE: **85,000 M²**

A MAGNOLIA ROOF

When the second phase of the Qi Zhong International Tennis Center is completed there will be forty courts in total, making it the largest tennis facility in Asia. Striking due to its eight-piece roof that resembles the petals of a blooming flower when open, the Center Court seats 15,000 people on its four floors. Built to stage the Tennis Masters Cup Shanghai, the retractable roof—that takes eight minutes to completely open or close—is ideal for playing in all seasons and can even be adapted for other sports such as basketball, volleyball, ping pang, and gymnastics. A tension-ring structure is used inside the stadium to create its coliseum-like form with reinforcement steel used both inside and outside the concrete. Below each seat an air-conditioning outlet regulates the temperature, while twenty broadcasting rooms allow simultaneous television coverage to a multitude of different media groups.

MAGNOLIENDACH

Das Qi Zhong International Tennis Center ist die größte Tennisanlage Asiens: Nach Beendigung der zweiten Bauphase werden insgesamt 40 Tennisplätze zur Verfügung stehen. Der Center Court, dessen beeindruckendes achtteiliges Dach im offenen Zustand an eine aufblühende Blume erinnert, nimmt auf vier Rängen bis zu 15.000 Besucher auf. Die Anlage wird als Austragungsort für den Tennis Master Cup Shanghai errichtet, die flexible Dachkonstruktion – es dauert nur acht Minuten, bis das Dach komplett geöffnet oder geschlossen ist – macht die Haupthalle darüber hinaus zu allen Jahreszeiten für Spiele nutzbar. Neben Tennis ist der Bau auch für Basketball-, Volleyball-, Tischtennis- oder Sportgymnastik-Veranstaltungen geeignet. Eine Spannring-Konstruktion aus Stahlbeton und Stahl verläuft um das Hauptstadion und verleiht ihm eine kolosseumähnliche Atmosphäre. Unter den Besuchersitzen verborgene modernste Klimatechnik sorgt für die Regelung der Temperaturen und von 20 Studios aus können simultane Live-Übertragungen gesendet werden.

1 THE CENTER COURT IS PART OF THE STILL TO BE COMPLETED QI ZHONG INTERNATIONAL TENNIS CENTER, WHICH WAS INSPIRED BY WIMBLEDON AND ROLAND GARROS.
DER CENTER COURT IST TEIL DES IM BAU BEFINDLICHEN QI ZHONG INTERNATIONAL TENNIS CENTER, DAS VON WIMBLEDON UND ROLAND GARROS ANGEREGT WURDE.
4 THE 15,050 SQUARE METER ROOF OF THE CENTER COURT WAS MODELED ON A MAGNOLIA, SHANGHAI'S OFFICIAL CITY FLOWER. EACH OF THE EIGHT "PETALS" WEIGHS TWO TONS.
DAS 15.050 QUADRATMETER GROSSE DACH DES CENTER COURTS IST EINER MAGNOLIE – SHANGHAIS OFFIZIELLER STADTBLUME – NACHEMPFUNDEN. JEDES DER ACHT »BLÜTENBLÄTTER« WIEGT ZWEI TONNEN.
3 APART FROM FEATURING THE TENNIS MASTERS CUP SHANGHAI, THE CENTER WILL BE HOME TO A FUTURE ACADEMY TO DEVELOP YOUNG TALENT.
DAS TENNISZENTRUM SOLL AUSTRAGUNGSORT DES TENNIS MASTER CUP SHANGHAI WERDEN, AUSSERDEM WIRD ES EINE TENNISAKADEMIE FÜR NACHWUCHSTALENTE BEHERBERGEN.
3 THE FOUR FLOORS MEASURE 40 METERS ABOVE GROUND LEVEL. 3,000 OF THE 15,000 SEATS ARE RESERVED FOR VIP'S AND ARE FOUND IN TWENTY-SIX DELUXE SKYBOXES AND COURTSIDE BOX SEATS.
DIE VIER BESUCHERRÄNGE LIEGEN IN 40 METERN HÖHE. 3.000 DER 15.000 PLÄTZE SIND FÜR VIP-GÄSTE RESERVIERT UND AUF 26 LUXURIÖSE KABINEN UND BOXEN VERTEILT.

REEBOK FLAGSHIP STORE

ARCHITECTS ARCHITEKTEN: CONTEMPORARY ARCHITECTURE PRACTICE

YEAR OF COMPLETION FERTIGSTELLUNG: 2007

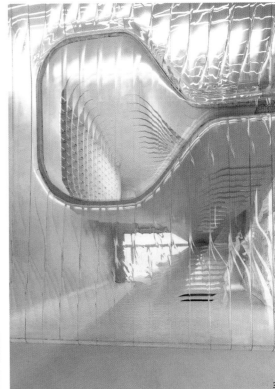

BRAND AS SPACE

The central theme of the design for the Reebok Flagship Store in Shanghai, provided by the New York Office of Contemporary Architecture Practice, is the brand itself. A large, walk-through logo—a three-dimensional manifestation of the slogan "Wear the Vector. Outperform"—will offer the visitor an entirely new shopping experience. The store is divided into three levels and outfitted in white fiberglass, which is occasionally substituted by transparent plastic surfaces. The organic form of the room's concept and its flexible lighting system impart a feeling of movement and speed. The various encased elements can be used in a number of ways, from presenting merchandise to seating options for customers and advertising space. Depending on the occasion, the space can even serve as a stage without weakening its unique character.

MARKE ALS RAUM

Zentrales Thema des Entwurfs für den Reebok Flagship Store Shanghai, vorgelegt vom New Yorker Büro Contemporary Architecture Practice, ist die Marke selbst. Ein begehbares Logo, eine dreidimensionale Manifestation des Slogans »Wear the Vector. Outperform« soll dem Kunden völlig neue Einkaufserlebnisse bieten. Der Shop, in drei Ebenen gegliedert, ist mit weißem, glasfaserverstärktem Kunststoff ausgekleidet, das an manchen Stellen von transparenten Kunststoffflächen durchbrochen wird. Die organischen Formen des Raumkonzepts und ein flexibles Beleuchtungssystem vermitteln Bewegung und Geschwindigkeit. Die in die Verkleidung eingearbeiteten Elemente sind variabel nutzbar, zur Präsentation von Artikeln, als Sitzmöglichkeiten für Kunden oder Werbefläche: je nach Anlass kann der Raum wie eine Bühne bespielt werden, ohne an Individualität zu verlieren.

1 THE ORGANIC FORMS OF THE REEBOK FLAGSHIP STORE ALLOW FOR MANY ASSOCIATIONS, FROM VISIBLE AIR CURRENTS TO WIND-BLOWN WATER SURFACES.
DIE ORGANISCHEN FORMEN DES REEBOK FLAGSHIP STORES LASSEN ZAHLREICHE ASSOZIATIONEN ZU, VON SICHTBAR GEMACHTEN LUFTSTRÖMUNGEN BIS ZUR GEKRÄUSELTEN WASSEROBERFLÄCHE.
2 THE DISPLAY AREAS ARE DIVIDED INTO VARIOUS LEVELS.
DER VERKAUFSRAUM IST IN MEHRERE EBENEN UNTERTEILT.
3 TRANSPARENT PLASTIC ELEMENTS AERATE THE FLOOR PLAN CONCEPT.
TRANSPARENTE KUNSTSTOFFELEMENTE LOCKERN DAS RAUMKONZEPT AUF.

NEW ICON

Reaching almost half a kilometer into the sky over Liujiazui the Shanghai World Financial Center—with its 101 floors—will be one of the highest skyscrapers in the world when completed. While the foundation stone was laid on August 27, 1997 construction only resumed in late 2005 after the project was stopped due to the Asian financial crises. The elongated tower with a square portal at its upper levels will contain offices, a luxury hotel with 300 rooms, retail and dining facilities, as well as an observation deck totaling more than 700 square meters. Financed by several multinational firms and banks the tower is bound to become a major symbol for the economic growth taken place both in Shanghai and China as a whole.

NEUE IKONE

Mit 101 Stockwerken und einer Höhe von fast einem halben Kilometer wird das World Financial Center im Finanzdistrikt Liujiazui in Pudong eines der höchsten Häuser der Welt sein. Die Arbeiten an dem Wolkenkratzer waren nach der Grundsteinlegung am 27. August 1997 aufgrund der Asienkrise zunächst gestoppt worden. Erst 2005 nahm man das Projekt wieder in Angriff. Der elegant aufragende Bau mit seiner trapezförmigen Öffnung im obersten Abschnitt wird neben Büros, einem Luxushotel mit 300 Zimmern, Läden und gastronomische Einrichtungen auch eine über 700 Quadratmeter große Aussichtsplattform beherbergen. Der von mehreren internationalen Banken und Firmen finanzierte Turm soll ein gebautes Symbol des wirtschaftlichen Wachstums sowohl Shanghais als auch Chinas werden.

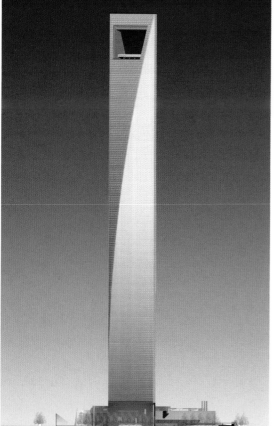

1 THE TOWER WILL DWARF THE ADJACENT JIN MAO BUILDING, AND IS SURE TO BECOME THE NEW ICON ON SHANGHAI'S SKYLINE.
DER WOLKENKRATZER WIRD DEN BENACHBARTEN JIN MAO TOWER ÜBERRAGEN UND EINE NEUE IKONE IN DER SKYLINE SHANGHAIS WERDEN.
2 WITH A HEIGHT OF 492 METERS THE TOWER WILL BE ONE OF THE TALLEST IN THE WORLD.
MIT 492 METERN WIRD DER TURM EINES DER HÖCHSTEN GEBÄUDE DER WELT SEIN.
3 THE SQUARE PRISM WAS CHANGED FROM THE EARLIER CIRCLE DESIGN, AND IS SAID TO REPRESENT THE EARTH IN ANCIENT CHINESE CULTURE.
DER DURCHBRUCH, DESSEN TRAPEZFORM IN DER CHINESISCHEN KULTUR DIE ERDE SYMBOLISIERT, ERSETZT FRÜHERE ENTWÜRFE EINES KREISRUNDEN LOCHES.

SHANGHAI WORLD
FINANCIAL CENTER

ARCHITECTS ARCHITEKTEN: **KOHN PEDERSON FOX ASSOCIATES**
YEAR OF COMPLETION FERTIGSTELLUNG: **2008**
AREA FLÄCHE: **377,300 M²**
HEIGHT HÖHE: **492 M**

KALEIDOSCOPIC GLAMOUR

TMSK serves as an excellent example of how modern art is being integrated into everyday life in Shanghai. Located in the popular Xintiandi district, Tou Ming Si Kao (TMSK), which translates into "transparent thinking," is a restaurant located in a traditional Shanghaiese building made of gray bricks and wooden-frame windows. The interior, however, is vastly different in style and feel. Conceived by two artists, the husband and wife team Loretta Hui-shan Yang, a former Taiwan actress, and Chang Yi, a former Taiwan director, TMSK is a space made almost entirely out of colored glass. The amalgamation of the art of *liuli* (glazed glass) and international culinary arts has been celebrated by locals and tourists alike.

GLAMOURÖSES KALEIDOSKOP

TMSK ist ein herausragendes Beispiel für die Integration moderner Kunst in das Alltagsbild Shanghais. Das Restaurant, dessen Name Tou Ming Si Kao (TMSK) übersetzt soviel bedeutet wie »transparentes Denken«, liegt im hippen Bezirk Xintiandi. Von außen ein traditioneller Shanghaier Grauziegelbau mit hölzernen Fensterrahmen, überrascht das Innere durch einen völlig anderen Stil. Loretta Hui-shan Yang, eine ehemalige Schauspielerin und Chang Yi, einst als Regisseur tätig – beide aus Taiwan und miteinander verheiratet – entwarfen in Teamarbeit das Raumkonzept des TMSK, das fast vollständig aus farbigem Glas besteht. Die Fusion aus moderner Interpretation von *liuli* (klassischer chinesischer Glaskunst) und internationaler Gastronomie erfreut sich sowohl bei Einheimischen als auch bei Touristen größter Beliebtheit.

1 UNASSUMING FROM THE OUTSIDE, TMSK LOOKS RELATIVELY CONSERVATIVE TO PASSERS-BY.
DAS BESCHEIDENE ÄUSSERE DES TMSK WIRKT ZURÜCKHALTEND.
2 ILLUMINATED RED, BAROQUE STYLE BAR STOOLS COMPLIMENT THE EMERALD GREEN BAR.
DIE ROT ERLEUCHTETEN BARHOCKER IM BAROCKEN STIL KONTRASTIEREN MIT DER SMARAGDGRÜNEN BAR.
3 SHANGHAI GLAMOUR ABOUNDS IN THE MAIN DINING ROOM.
IM RESTAURANTBEREICH DOMINIERT SHANGHAIER GLAMOUR.
4 *LIULI*, OR GLAZED GLASS, HAS HELPED TO MAKE TMSK A MUST-SEE IN SHANGHAI.
CHINESISCHE GLASKUNST, *LIULI*, MACHT DAS TMSK ZU EINEM HÖHEPUNKT SHANGHAIS.
5 TMSK IS EQUAL PARTS RESTAURANT, BAR, AND WORK OF ART.
TMSK IST NICHT NUR BAR UND RESTAURANT, SONDERN GLEICHZEITIG KUNSTWERK.

TMSK

ARCHITECTS ARCHITEKTEN: LORETTA HUI-SHAN YANG AND CHANG YI

YEAR OF COMPLETION FERTIGSTELLUNG: 2001

TOMORROW SQUARE

ARCHITECTS ARCHITEKTEN: **JOHN PORTMAN & ASSOCIATES, INC.**

YEAR OF COMPLETION FERTIGSTELLUNG: **2003**

AREA FLÄCHE: **93,153 M²**

HEIGHT HÖHE: **285 M**

1 ITS UNIQUE FORM SETS THE BUILDING OFF FROM ITS URBAN CONTEXT.
DIE PRÄGNANTE FORM HEBT DAS GEBÄUDE VON SEINER UMGEBUNG AB.
2 THE STRUCTURE DOMINATES THE SURROUNDING PEOPLE'S SQUARE. AT NIGHT, TOMORROW
SQUARE SHINES ABOVE SHANGHAI'S SEA OF BUILDINGS.
DER BAU DOMINIERT DIE GEGEND UM DEN PLATZ DES VOLKES: NACHTS STRAHLT DER TOMORROW
SQUARE VOR DEM HÄUSERMEER SHANGHAIS.
3 FOLDED, GEOMETRIC FORMS AND CLEAR LINES DEFINE THE ARCHITECTURE OF THIS BUILDING.
GEOMETRISCHE FORMEN, INEINANDER VERSCHACHTELT: KLARE LINIEN BESTIMMEN DIE ARCHITEKTUR.
4 THE ELEVATOR-LOBBY—UNADULTERATED INTERIOR DESIGN WITH DELICATE DETAILS.
DIE AUFZUG-LOBBY: PURISTISCHE INNENGESTALTUNG MIT FEINEN DETAILS.

THE BUILT FUTURE

The name stands for its function: a building for the future. Located directly on the People's Square and near one of the most important shopping streets, Nanjing Xi Lu, the 60 floor central building of Tomorrow Square seems like a futuristic monolith. The Marriott Group rents the lower level apartments to business people, the upper levels—visually separated by way of a 45 degree twist of the quadratic foundation plan—are occupied by the 342-room Marriot hotel. The pinnacle of the building, with its free-standing triangular forms, marks the skyline with its unique sculptural form and marks Tomorrow Square as one of the architectural landmarks of the city.

GEBAUTE ZUKUNFT

Der Name ist Programm bei dieser Gebäudeanlage im Herzen Shanghais: Direkt am Platz des Volkes und einer der wichtigsten Einkaufsstraßen, der Nanjing Xi Lu, gelegen, wirkt der 60 Stockwerke hohe Hauptbau des Tomorrow Square wie ein futuristischer Monolith. Die Marriott Gruppe vermietet im unteren Gebäudeteil Apartments für Geschäftsleute, die oberen Stockwerke – durch eine Drehung des quadratischen Grundrisses um 45 Grad optisch abgetrennt – beherbergen ein Marriot Hotel mit 342 Zimmern. Die durchbrochene Turmspitze prägt mit ihrer einzigartigen skulpturalen Form die Skyline und macht den Tomorrow Square zu einem architektonischen Wahrzeichen der Stadt.

SINGAPORE

● SINGAPORE

POPULATION EINWOHNERZAHL: **CA. 4,400,000 INCLUDING THE GREATER METROPOLITAN AREA**
INKLUSIVE METROPOLREGION

POPULATION DENSITY EINWOHNERDICHTE: **6,389 PERSONS PER KM²**

AREA FLÄCHE: **682.7 KM² (MAIN ISLAND** HAUPTINSEL**), 692.7 KM² (TOTAL LAND AND WATER AREA**
LAND- UND WASSERFLÄCHE INSGESAMT**)**

WEBSITE: WWW.GOV.SG

Singapore is the second most densely populated independent country in the world. Its population of approximately 4.4 million is racially diverse and multi-religious. Singapore became a magnet for immigrants and merchants during its years as a British trading post and currently consists of seventy-seven percent Chinese, fourteen percent Malay, eight percent Indian and one percent of other descents. There are four official languages in Singapore: Malay, Mandarin, Tamil, and English; most Singaporeans are bilingual. Racial harmony has been emphasized in all aspects of society including education, residential, and military. The various ethnic neighborhoods, once created to promote segregation, now thrive from a diverse patronage interested in foreign culture.

Die Republik Singapur ist der am zweitdichtesten besiedelte Staat der Welt. Die 4,4 Millionen Einwohner haben unterschiedlichste ethnische Hintergründe, dementsprechend vielfältig sind auch die Religionszugehörigkeiten. Als britische Kronkolonie übte Singapur große Anziehungskraft auf Immigranten und Geschäftsleute aus; heute setzt sich die Bevölkerung aus 77 Prozent Chinesen, 14 Prozent Malaien, acht Prozent Indern und einem Prozent anderen Volksgruppen zusammen. Es gibt vier Amtssprachen in Singapur: Malaiisch, Hochchinesisch, Tamil und Englisch, die meisten Singapurer sind zweisprachig. Die Eintracht zwischen den verschiedenen Volksgruppen spielt im sozialen Zusammenleben eine große Rolle und wird in allen Bereichen – beispielsweise Bildungswesen, Wohnraumverteilung oder Militär – betont und gefördert. Viertel mit ehemals ethnischen Schwerpunkten, einst bewusst forciert, erblühen heute in neuer kultureller Vielfalt.

Singapore is an island state located on the tip of the Malay Peninsula comprising one main island and around sixty-three offshore islands. Singapore was founded as a British trading colony in 1819, joined the Malaysian Federation in 1963, only to separate and become independent two years later. In 150 years, Singapore has evolved from a developing country to a highly developed industrialized one. Singapore has an advanced, market-based economy and is ranked 25th on the Human Development Index which measures standards of living. Singapore's strategic geographic position has lead to its strategic significance in matters of trade, communications, and tourism. The economy relies heavily on export and the city is home to the most active port in the world.

Singapur wurde 1819 als Niederlassung der Britischen Ostindischen Handelskompanie an einem alten Handelssitz gegründet. 1963 folgte der Beitritt in eine Föderation mit Malaysia, nur zwei Jahre später wurde die Unabhängigkeit erreicht. In einem Zeitraum von 150 Jahren wandelte sich Singapur vom Entwicklungs- zum hochentwickelten Industrieland: Die Republik hat eine florierende Marktwirtschaft und rangiert an 25. Stelle des Human Development Index, der als Messinstrument des Lebensstandards gilt. Singapur liegt am Südende der Malaiischen Halbinsel und besteht aus einer Haupt- sowie 63 kleineren Nebeninseln. Der Inselstaat belegt damit einen geografischen Knotenpunkt. Diese strategisch günstige Position wirkt sich positiv auf den Handel, die Infrastruktur und den Tourismus aus. Das Land ist eine Exportnation und betreibt den Hafen mit dem weltweit größten Handelsvolumen.

Since the 1980s, critics have called for a re-vamp of the city's "stoic" architecture. This, in turn, has lead to an increase in architectural styles, especially postmodernist and neoclassic. Today, the city is dominated by modern architecture. Since the 1990s, the government has been striving to promote Singapore as a center for art and culture, and to transform the country into a cosmopolitan community. The highlight of these efforts opened in 2003: The Esplanades—Theaters on the Bay, a center for the performing arts.

Seit den 1980er Jahren haben Kritiker für eine Abkehr von den gängigen, eher nüchtern gehaltenen architektonischen Strukturen der Stadt plädiert. Dies wiederum führte zu einer Diversifizierung der Stile, besonders postmoderne und neoklassizistische Entwürfe setzten sich durch. Heute wird die Stadt von moderner Architektur dominiert. Die Regierung bemüht sich seit den 1990er Jahren, Singapurs Status als Zentrum für Kunst und Kultur auszubauen. Der vorläufige Höhepunkt dieser Bestrebungen ist das 2003 eröffnete Konzert- und Theaterhaus The Esplanades.

ASSYAFAAH MOSQUE

ARCHITECTS ARCHITEKTEN: **FORUM ARCHITECTS**
YEAR OF COMPLETION FERTIGSTELLUNG: **2005**

1 THE ASSYAFAAH MOSQUE FASCINATES IN ITS MODERNITY AND ITS ABANDONMENT OF TRADITIONAL ELEMENTS.
DIE ASSYAFAAH MOSCHEE BESTICHT DURCH IHRE MODERNITÄT UND DEN VERZICHT AUF TRADITIONELLE ELEMENTE.
2 NATURAL LIGHT AND WHITE SURFACES CREATE AN ATMOSPHERE OF PURITY.
GROSSZÜGIGER LICHTEINFALL UND WEISSE FLÄCHEN SCHAFFEN EINE ATMOSPHÄRE DER REINHEIT.
3 MINARET AS SCULPTURE—LIKE A PILLAR, THE STEEL-PLATE STRUCTURE RISES INTO THE CLOUDS.
MINARETT ALS SKULPTUR: WIE EINE SÄULE RAGT DIE STAHLPLATTEN-KONSTRUKTION IN DEN HIMMEL.

AIRY SANCTUM

The Singapore-based practice, Forum Architects, has ventured a break with tradition in their design for the Assyafaah Mosque. In order to meet the requirements of the city-state's multifarious population, as well as providing for the divergent cultural aspects within the Islamic faith, the architects avoided using typical elements—a cupola for instance—to give the building a modern and neutral appearance. Due to the high humidity and tropical temperatures, closed rooms were largely avoided. Open, arabesque-shaped aluminum screens allow for the appropriate amount of air circulation as well as an almost visual dematerialization of the walls.

OFFENES HAUS

Einen Bruch mit den Traditionen wagte das in Singapur ansässige Architekturbüro Forum Architects mit dem Entwurf der Assyafaah Moschee: Um der ethnisch komplexen Zusammensetzung des Stadtstaates und den divergierenden kulturellen Hintergründen der islamischen Gläubigen gerecht zu werden, verzichtet der Bau auf herkömmliche Elemente wie beispielsweise eine Kuppel, und hat stattdessen ein modernes, sachliches Erscheinungsbild. Aufgrund der hohen Luftfeuchtigkeit und den tropischen Temperaturen wurde zu großen Teilen auf geschlossenes Mauerwerk verzichtet: Offene, aus Arabesken geformte Aluminium-Gitterstrukturen ermöglichen nicht nur die nötige Luftzirkulation, sondern sorgen gleichzeitig für eine visuelle Entmaterialisierung der Wände.

THE ESPLANADES

ARCHITECTS ARCHITEKTEN: MICHAEL WILFORD & PARTNERS, DP ARCHITECTS
YEAR OF COMPLETION FERTIGSTELLUNG: 2002
AREA FLÄCHE: 75,186 M²

SHINING STAR

The cultural center "The Esplanades"—in Marina Park, situated between Marina Center and Marina Bay—has enriched the skyline of Singapore since 2002. The structure, named "durian" (a local fruit) by the locals due to its distinctive shell of triangular, isolating glass panels, covers over four hectares and contains much more than just venue space, namely practice rooms, a shopping mall, a restaurant, administrative offices, as well as apartments. The Center hosts a wide range of artistic activities presented in its five concert and theater auditoriums with seating capacities from 250 to 1,800. Additionally, the area has invested in more open-air theater space for outdoor performances.

STRAHLENDER STERN

Das Kulturzentrum The Esplanades – im Marina Park, zwischen Marina Center und Marina Bay gelegen – bereichert seit 2002 die Skyline Singapurs. Die Anlage, die von den Einheimischen wegen ihrer markanten Hülle aus Dreiecks-Isolierglasscheiben auch »Durian« (Stinkfrucht) genannt wird, erstreckt sich über vier Hektar und ist nicht nur Veranstaltungsort, sondern beherbergt ebenso Proberäume, eine Shopping Mall, ein Restaurant, Verwaltungsbüros und sogar Apartments. Das Zentrum bietet auf den Bühnen seiner insgesamt fünf Konzert- und Theatersäle, deren Kapazitäten von 250 bis 1.800 Plätze reichen, ein breites Spektrum künstlerischer Aktivitäten. Auf dem Areal wurden darüber hinaus mehrere Freilichtbühnen angelegt, die für Open-Air-Aufführungen zur Verfügung stehen.

1 AT NIGHT, THE GLOWING STRUCTURE TURNS INTO A REAL EYE-CATCHER.
NACHTS WIRD DER BELEUCHTETE BAU ZUM BLICKFANG.
2 THE UNIQUE GLASS SHELL OF THE CULTURAL CENTER IS REMINISCENT OF THE FRUIT OF THE DURIAN TREE, SIMILAR TO THE PINEAPPLE.
DIE EIGENWILLIGE GLASHÜLLE DES KULTURZENTRUMS ERINNERT AN DIE ANANASÄHNLICHE FRUCHT DES DURIANBAUMES.
3 THE GLASS STRUCTURE GIVES THE BUILDING A CERTAIN TRANSPARENCY.
DIE GLASSTRUKTUR VERLEIHT DEM BAU TRANSPARENZ.
4 A TOTAL OF FIVE, VARIOUSLY SIZED HALLS CAN BE USED FOR PERFORMANCES.
INSGESAMT FÜNF SÄLE UNTERSCHIEDLICHER GRÖSSE KÖNNEN BESPIELT WERDEN.

HOVERING STATION

Providing access to the massive 100,000 square-meter Singapore Expo Center via the MRT (Mass Rapid Transit) Changi Airport Line, this spaceship-like train station was built with the region's extremely warm temperatures in mind. The two titanium-clad, overlapping roof elements—a forty meter-diameter round disk and a 130 meter-long elliptical form—allow cooling air to flow through the building while the reflective panels underneath minimize the need for artificial lighting. The external cladding deflects the sun's rays, thereby creating a micro-climate on the platforms that is up to four degrees cooler than the outside temperature. The elegant design, so characteristic for the Foster Studio, allows for clear sightlines throughout the station, which is useful for orientation during busy fare times.

SCHWEBENDE STATION

Diese Haltestelle der MRT (Mass Rapid Transit) Changi Airport Line gehört zum 100.000 Quadratmeter großen Singapore Expo Center. Der raumschiffartige Entwurf liegt in den extrem warmen Temperaturen der Region begründet: Die zwei titanverkleideten Dächer, die sich teil-weise überlagern – eine Scheibe mit 40 Metern Durchmesser sowie eine 130 Meter lange elliptische Form – erlauben einen kühlenden Luftzug durch das Gebäude, die reflektierende Verkleidung der Dachunterseiten minimiert den Bedarf an künstlicher Beleuchtung. Die äußere Schale der Dächer lenkt die Sonnenstrahlen ab und schafft so ein Mikroklima auf dem Bahnsteig, dessen Temperaturen bis zu vier Grad niedriger liegen als außerhalb. Das elegante, für das Büro Foster and Partners charak-teristische Design kreiert klare Sichtachsen durch die Station, was die Orientierung gerade in den Stoßzeiten erleichtert.

EXPO MRT STATION

ARCHITECTS ARCHITEKTEN: **FOSTER AND PARTNERS**
YEAR OF COMPLETION FERTIGSTELLUNG: **2001**

THE SAIL@MARINA BAY

ARCHITECTS ARCHITEKTEN: PETER PRAN / NBBJ
YEAR OF COMPLETION FERTIGSTELLUNG: 2009
AREA FLÄCHE: 9,090.9 M²

1 CLAD IN TRANSPARENT GLASS, THE TOWER'S SCULPTED EXTERIOR GIVES THE APPEARANCE OF BEING FORMED BY WATER.
DIE GLÄSERNEN FASSADEN DER TÜRME WIRKEN WIE VON WASSER GEFORMT.
2 TOWER RESIDENTS WILL BE ABLE TO ENJOY OPULENT VIEWS OF THE MARINA BAY AND CITY CENTER, WHILE THOSE LIVING IN ONE OF THE FIVE PENTHOUSES CAN TAKE IN THE SEA AND THE ISLANDS BEYOND.
DIE BEWOHNER DER ANLAGE WERDEN EINEN PANORAMABLICK ÜBER DIE MARINA BAY UND DAS STADTZENTRUM GENIESSEN KÖNNEN, VON DEN FÜNF PENTHÄUSERN AUS SIND SOGAR DAS MEER UND WEITER ENTFERNT LIEGENDE INSELN SICHTBAR.
3 THE SAIL@MARINA BAY IS EXPECTED TO RANK AS ONE OF THE CITY'S TOP LANDMARKS.
DER SAIL@MARINA BAY-KOMPLEX SOLL EINES DER WICHTIGSTEN WAHRZEICHEN DER STADT WERDEN.
4 AN ARCHITECTURAL "CANYON" THAT SEPARATES THE TWO TOWERS FROM THE BASE EXPOSES A GREEN, URBAN SPACE.
DIE ARCHITEKTONISCHE SCHLUCHT ZWISCHEN DEN BEIDEN TÜRMEN IST AM BODEN MIT EINER GRÜNFLÄCHE BEDECKT.

ELEMENTAL GIANT

This pivotal project in the Urban Renewal Authority's plan to spruce up Singapore's Central Business District waterfront is targeted to set a new benchmark for an integrated lifestyle environment. The Sail@Marina Bay, soon to be the area's tallest structure at 245 meters high, is destined to become one of the city's landmarks. Among the top ten tallest residential building in the world, this luxury high-rise complex consists of two dominant towers (Marina Bay Tower: 70 floors and Central Park Tower: 63 floors) along with a sculpted base. Inspired by the elements fire, wind, and water, Peter Pran designed the complex to reflect a huge canyon in its entirety while the prominent tower resembles a sail catching the wind.

SPIEL DER ELEMENTE

Im Zuge des städtischen Erneuerungsplans, dessen Ziel die Modernisierung des am Ufer gelegenen Central Business Districts ist, setzt dieses Schlüsselprojekt neue Maßstäbe für die Vielseitigkeit des Geschäftsviertels: Das Sail@Marina Bay soll mit 245 Metern der höchste Bau Singapurs werden und gilt als ein zukünftiges Wahrzeichen der Stadt. Der luxuriöse Hochhauskomplex, der zu den zehn höchsten Wohngebäuden der Welt zählt, besteht aus zwei markanten Türmen (Marina Bay Tower: 70 Stockwerke und Central Park Tower: 63 Stockwerke) sowie einem Sockelbau. Inspiriert von den Elementen Feuer, Wind und Wasser, entwarf der Architekt Peter Pran die Anlage zum einen in Anspielung an eine große Schlucht, zum anderen erinnert der höhere Turm an ein im Wind geblähtes Segel.

OLD AND NEW

Designed by Foster and Partners, one of the most prolific architectural practices in the world, Singapore's newly-completed Supreme Court building stands in the Colonial District opposite its forerunner from 1939. Housing twelve civil, eight criminal, and three appellate courts with its highest court—the Court of Appeal—raised symbolically over the others in a disc-like form, much care was taken to integrate the building into its urban context through its modern, open appearance. The nine-floor building, flanked by administrative office blocks, was built in an assortment of high-quality materials, including a semi-transparent laminate of glass and stone along with hand-picked marble from Italy. Trees planted along the rims of the blocks provide shade for the public promenade. Similar to the cupola that Norman Foster's designed for the German Reichstag, the Court of Appeal also includes a viewing platform that is open to the public.

ALT UND NEU

Foster and Partners, eines der weltweit produktivsten Architekturbüros, entwarf den kürzlich fertig gestellten Neubau des Supreme Court, errichtet gegenüber dem Vorgängerbau aus dem Jahr 1939 im Colonial District Singapurs. Der Bau beherbergt zwölf Zivilgerichte, acht Strafgerichte sowie drei Berufungsgerichte, zu denen auch das höchste Gericht – der Court of Appeal – zählt, das als symbolträchtiger Rundbau über dem gesamten Komplex thront. Der Supreme Court mit seiner bewusst modernen, offenen Anlage wurde umsichtig in den urbanen Kontext integriert. Für das neunstöckige, von Bürobauten flankierte Gebäude wurden hochwertige Materialien verwendet, unter anderem ein halbtransparenter Verbund aus Glas und Stein sowie sorgfältig ausgewählter italienischer Marmor. Um den Bau herum gepflanzte Bäume spenden Schatten für die öffentlichen Gehwege. Wie die von Foster entworfene Kuppel des Reichstages in Berlin, bietet auch der Court of Appeal eine Aussichtsplattform, die für Besucher offen ist.

1 THE NEW SUPREME COURT STRIKES A FINE BALANCE BETWEEN COLONIAL DISTRICT AND HIGH-RISE DEVELOPMENTS BEYOND IT ON THE SOUTH SIDE OF THE SINGAPORE RIVER.
DER NEUE SUPREME COURT IST EIN ARCHITEKTONISCHES BINDEGLIED ZWISCHEN DEM COLONIAL DISTRICT UND DEN HOCHHAUSBAUTEN AM SÜDUFER DES SINGAPUR-FLUSSES.
2 THE SPACESHIP-LIKE DISK ITERATES THE CLASSICAL DOME OF THE OLD SUPREME COURT TO THE RIGHT.
DIE AN EIN RAUMSCHIFF ERINNERNDE RUNDE FORM IST EIN WIDERHALL DER KUPPEL DES ALTEN SUPREME COURT AUF DER RECHTEN SEITE.
3 A VIEW INTO THE CENTRAL ATRIUM WITH THE ESCALATORS LEADING TO THE UPPER FLOORS.
EIN BLICK IN DAS ZENTRALE ATRIUM MIT ROLLTREPPEN, DIE IN DIE OBEREN STOCKWERKE FÜHREN.
4 THE LAMINATE OF GLASS AND STONE ALLOWS LIGHT TO FILTER INTO THE BUILDING. AT NIGHT IT GIVES OFF A WARM GLOW.
DER VERBUND AUS GLAS UND STEIN ERLAUBT LICHTEINFALL IN DAS GEBÄUDE. NACHTS GEHT EIN WARMES LEUCHTEN VON DEM BAU AUS.

SUPREME COURT

ARCHITECTS ARCHITEKTEN: **FOSTER AND PARTNERS**

YEAR OF COMPLETION FERTIGSTELLUNG: **2006**

TAIPEI

TAIPEI

POPULATION EINWOHNERZAHL: CA. 2,700,000
POPULATION DENSITY EINWOHNERDICHTE: 9,735 PERSONS PER KM²
AREA FLÄCHE: 272 KM²
WEBSITE: HTTP://ENGLISH.TAIPEI.GOV.TW

「TAIWAN 113」

Taipei is the capital of the Republic of China on the island of Taiwan, a country that is officially recognized by only a few states. The development of the city started at the beginning of the eighteenth century and it became the capital in 1949 when the government of China retreated to the island from the Maoists who occupied the mainland. Today Taipei is the political, business, and cultural center of the state. Over two and a half million people live in the city's twelve districts, more than ten percent of the total population of Taiwan. If one includes the surrounding communities and the illegal immigrants then the figure is over five million. Although in comparison with other Asian cities Taipei is not a highly populated metropolitan region, it still ranks among the top ten as far as competitiveness and quality of life are concerned

Taipeh ist die Hauptstadt der nur von wenigen Staaten politisch anerkannten Republik China auf der Insel Taiwan. Die Stadtentwicklung beginnt Anfang des 18. Jahrhunderts, die Ernennung zur Hauptstadt erfolgte 1949, als sich die Regierung Chinas vor den Maoisten vom Festland auf die Insel zurückzog. Heute ist Taipeh das politische, wirtschaftliche und kulturelle Zentrum des Staates. In seinen zwölf Stadtteilen leben über zweieinhalb Millionen Menschen, mehr als 10 Prozent der Gesamtbevölkerung Taiwans. Zählt man die umliegenden Gemeinden und illegalen Zuwanderer hinzu, liegt die Zahl bei über fünf Millionen. Zwar gehört Taipeh damit zu keiner der Metropolregionen mit extrem hoher Bevölkerungszahl, es rangiert aber hinsichtlich Wettbewerbsfähigkeit und Lebensqualität im Vergleich mit anderen asiatischen Städten unter den ersten Zehn.

One fifth of Taiwanese businesses are located in Taipei, which is where two-thirds of Taiwan's goods and services are produced and provided. Over 75 percent of the companies operate in the commercial and financial sector and almost 80 percent of all employees work in service industries. There are sixteen universities with many different faculties and indeed the high level of education is one of Taipei's main advantages in the Asian area. The city is currently in a state of change: in addition to the traditionally strong field of industrial production, research and development in the information and biotechnology sectors are beginning to play a more important role. For many European and US firms Taipei represents an ideal gateway to the mainland China market.

In Taipeh befindet sich ein Fünftel der taiwanesischen Unternehmen, hier werden über zwei Drittel der Güter und Dienstleistungen Taiwans erwirtschaftet. Über 75 Prozent der Betriebe gehören zum Handel- und Finanzsektor, fast 80 Prozent der Beschäftigten arbeiten im Dienstleistungsbereich. Sechzehn Universitäten bilden Studenten aller Fakultäten aus, das hohe Bildungsniveau ist einer der Hauptstandortvorteile Taipehs im asiatischen Raum. Die Stadt befindet sich im Umbruch, neben der traditionell starken industriellen Produktion nehmen nun Forschung und Entwicklung im Informations- und Biotechnologie-Sektor einen immer breiteren Raum ein. Für viele europäische und US-amerikanische Firmen stellt Taipeh das ideale Portal zum chinesischen Festlandsmarkt dar.

With the comprehensive subsidization of the public local transport system and the MRT (Mass Rapid Transit), a rapid urban railway system, the city has been able to ensure the necessary mobility of workers and goods as well as to considerably improve the quality of the air and of life in general. The large shopping centers that are developing throughout the city offer a further sign of urban development and improvement. The largest among them so far, the avant-garde Core Pacific City with over 1,000 shops, attracted 300,000 people on the day it opened. In the area of urban planning terms Taipei is increasingly beginning to focus on green areas. Not only are the luxuriant mountain forests of Beitou, Shilin, Neihu, and Nangan being opened up as local recreation and leisure time areas, but the inner city banks of the rivers Keelung, Shuangxi, and Jingmei are being developed into green recreation islands for city dwellers.

Mit einer umfassenden Förderung des Öffentlichen Personennahverkehrs und der MRT (Mass Rapid Transit), einem städtischen Schnellbahnsystem, gelang es der Stadt, die nötige Dynamik und Mobilität der Arbeitnehmer und Güter zu gewährleisten, sowie die Luft- und Lebensqualität deutlich zu erhöhen. Ein weiteres Kennzeichen der urbanen Aufwärtsentwicklung sind die großen Einkaufszentren, die sich in der Stadt ausbreiten. Das bislang größte unter ihnen, die avantgardistische *Core Pacific City* mit über 1000 Geschäften, zog am Eröffnungstag 300.000 Menschen an. Stadtplanerisch werden nun auch die Grünflächen in den Fokus genommen. Nicht nur sollen die angrenzenden üppigen Bergwälder von Beitou, Shilin, Neihu und Nangan als Naherholungsgebiete erschlossen werden, auch die innerstädtischen Ufer der Flussläufe des Keelung, Shuangxi und Jingmei werden nun zu grünen Erholungsinseln für die Stadtbewohner ausgebaut.

BACK TO NATURE

Harmony between high-tech, man, and nature is at the core of the designs produced by tec architecture. This is illustrated in the unusual quality of the Inotera Headquarters complex, which was erected in an industrial park on the periphery of Taipei. The office building with the adjoining microchip production hall is lent an almost romantic quality by its diversity of forms and colors and contrasts like an exotic bird of paradise with its mundane built environment. The colorful glass facade of the office wing is made up of small parts created by means of a new process that allows glass to be printed according to computer-generated originals. It shimmers in different shades of color according to the incidence of light and the standpoint of the viewer, while the pattern of the blue tiles on the outside walls of the production building helps to visually shorten the facade.

ZURÜCK ZUR NATUR

Die Harmonie zwischen Hightech, Mensch und Natur ist Kern der Entwürfe des Architekturbüros tec architecture. Entsprechend unge-wöhnlich ist der Gebäudekomplex der Inotera Headquarters, der in einem Industriepark am Rande Taipehs errichtet wurde. Das Büro-gebäude mit angegliederter Mikrochip-Produktionshalle hat mit seiner Vielfalt von Farben und Formen eine geradezu romantische Anmutung und hebt sich von der baulichen Umgebung ab wie ein schillernder Paradiesvogel. Die kleinteilige, bunte Glasfassade des Bürotrakts – hergestellt mit einem neuen Verfahren, das es erlaubt, Glas nach computergenerierten Vorgaben zu bedrucken – schimmert je nach Lichteinfall und Betrachterstandpunkt in unterschiedlichen Farbtönen, die blauen Fliesen an den Außenwänden der Fertigungshalle ist sind so gemustert, dass die Fassade optisch verkürzt wirkt.

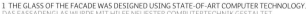

1 THE GLASS OF THE FACADE WAS DESIGNED USING STATE-OF-ART COMPUTER TECHNOLOGY.
DAS FASSADENGLAS WURDE MIT HILFE NEUESTER COMPUTERTECHNIK GESTALTET.
2 ADMINISTRATION AND PRODUCTION LIE SIDE BY SIDE. THE DESIGNS OF THE DIFFERENT FACADES OPTICALLY SEPARATE THE INDIVIDUAL BUILDINGS.
VERWALTUNG UND PRODUKTION LIEGEN NEBENEINANDER. DIE UNTERSCHIEDLICHE FASSADEN-GESTALTUNG TRENNT DIE GEBÄUDETEILE OPTISCH.
3 THE SLANTED COLUMNS STAND IN CONTRAST TO THE RIGHT ANGLES OF THE FACADE.
DIE SCHRÄGEN STÜTZEN STEHEN IN SPANNUNGSREICHEM KONTRAST ZU DEN RECHTEN WINKELN DER FASSADE.
4 COLORED GLASS AND TILES PROVIDE THE INOTERA HEADQUARTERS WITH AN INDIVIDUAL NOTE.
BUNTES GLAS UND VERSCHIEDENFARBIGE FLIESEN VERLEIHEN DEM BAU DER INOTERA HEADQUARTERS EINE INDIVIDUELLE NOTE.

INOTERA HEADQUARTERS

ARCHITECTS ARCHITEKTEN: **TEC ARCHITECTURE**
YEAR OF COMPLETION FERTIGSTELLUNG: **2005**
AREA FLÄCHE: **26,900 M² OFFICE SPACE** BÜROS; **18,600 M² PRODUCTION SPACE** PRODUKTION

KUO HUA INSURANCE BUILDING

LIGHT ARCHITECTURE LICHTARCHITEKTUR: **TIRSYS**
INSTALLATION INSTALLATION: **2004**
HEIGHT HÖHE: **16 FLOORS** STOCKWERKE

1 AT NIGHT THE BUILDING OF THE KUO HUA INSURANCE SHIMMERS IN THE COLORS OF THE
RAINBOW—THANKS TO THE USE OF SOPHISTICATED LIGHTING TECHNOLOGY.
NACHTS SCHILLERT DAS GEBÄUDE DER KUO HUA INSURANCE DANK AUSGEKLÜGELTER
BELEUCHTUNGSTECHNIK IN REGENBOGENFARBEN.
2 SPECIAL SCREENS TRANSFORM THE WINDOWS INTO LIGHT BOXES.
SPEZIELLE BLENDEN ERMÖGLICHEN DIE WANDLUNG VOM FENSTER ZUM LEUCHTKASTEN.
3 THE LIGHT BOXES CAN BE INDIVIDUALLY PROGRAMMED.
DIE LEUCHTKÄSTEN SIND INDIVIDUELL PROGRAMMIERBAR.

COLORFUL CHECKERBOARD

The Kuo Hua Insurance building in the inner city of Taipei is an opalescent
example of the undreamt of opportunities that solid-state lighting offers
for facade design. During the daytime light enters the offices of the insurance company through normal glass windows, but with the onset
of dusk screens with a reflective surface slide automatically across
the windowpanes, transforming them into light boxes. Each window
becomes one of a total of 220 "color pixels" that can be individually
programmed in terms of the sequence in which they are illuminated
and the colors used. The dynamic night-time illumination of the facade
changes constantly, becoming a "highlight" of the architectural use of
light, in the truest sense of the word.

BUNTES SCHACHBRETT

Das Gebäude der Kuo Hua Insurance in Taipehs Innenstadt ist ein
schillerndes Beispiel dafür, welche ungeahnten Möglichkeiten Fest-
körperbeleuchtung für die Fassadengestaltung bietet. Tagsüber fällt
durch normale Glasfenster Licht in die Büros der Versicherung, doch
mit Einsatz der Dämmerung schieben sich automatisch Blenden mit
reflektierender Oberfläche über die Scheiben und verwandeln diese in
Leuchtkästen. Jedes Fenster wird zu einem von insgesamt 220 »Farb-
pixeln«, deren Beleuchtungs- und Farbabfolge individuell programmierbar ist. Die Fassade erhält eine dynamische Nachtbeleuchtung, die
sich ständig wandelt und zu einem lichtarchitektonischen »Highlight«
im wahrsten Sinne des Wortes wird.

TAIPEI 101

ARCHITECTS ARCHITEKTEN: **C.Y. LEE AND PARTNERS**

YEAR OF COMPLETION FERTIGSTELLUNG: **2004**

AREA FLÄCHE: **412,500 M²**

THE WORLD'S TALLEST

Currently the tallest building in the world Taipei 101, named after its number of floors, is the major landmark of Taipei City. Originally named the Taipei Financial Center the building is 509 meters high and took five years to complete. Its exterior is made up of eight distinctive, bamboo stalk-like sections that are meant to represent gold ingots, while four circles on each side of the building are intended to represent coins. Designed to withstand earthquakes above seven on the Richter scale, the building is equipped with a total of 63 elevators which run at top speeds of 1,010 meters per minute. A vibration damper consisting of a suspended steel ball was installed on the 88th floor to stabilize the building during high winds. The building's interior—designed along *feng shui* lines—holds a six-floor retail mall with shops and restaurants and an observatory on the 91st floor provides dramatic views over downtown Taipei.

DER GRÖSSTE DER WELT

Taipei 101, das zur Zeit höchste Gebäude der Welt, ist nach der Anzahl seiner Stockwerke benannt und stellt das wichtigste Wahrzeichen Taipehs dar. Der ursprünglich Taipei Financial Center genannte Wolkenkratzer ist 509 Meter hoch und zu seiner Fertigstellung wurden fünf Jahre benötigt. Er besteht aus acht markanten Teilen, die an Bamusstängel erinnern, und Goldbarren darstellen sollen, während die vier Kreise, die jeweils an den Seiten des Gebäudes zu sehen sind, Münzen verkörpern. Die Konstruktion des Gebäudes ist darauf ausgelegt, Erdbeben der Stärke sieben und höher auf der Richterskala standzuhalten, eine freihängende Stahlkugel im 88. Stock stabilisiert als Schwingungsdämpfer das Gebäude bei starken Winden. 63 Aufzüge befördern die Mitarbeiter mit einer Rekordgeschwindigkeit von 1.010 Metern pro Sekunde. Das Innere des Gebäudes wurde nach Feng-Shui-Richtlinien gestaltet, auf sechs Geschossen ist ein Einkaufzentrum mit Geschäften und Restaurants untergebracht, im 91. Stock befindet sich eine Aussichtsplattform, die eine spektakuläre Aussicht über die Innenstadt von Taipeh bietet.

1 RESEMBLING A GIANT GLASS PAGODA, TAIPEI 101 IS THE HIGHEST BUILDING IN THE WORLD, 50 METERS HIGHER THAN THE PETRONAS TWIN TOWERS.
DAS TAIPEI 101 ERINNERT AN EINE RIESIGE GLASPAGODE UND IST DAS HÖCHSTE GEBÄUDE DER WELT, 50 METER HÖHER ALS DIE PETRONAS TWIN TOWERS.
2 WITH A WEIGHT OF 700,000 TONS TAIPEI 101 IS SO HEAVY THAT THERE ARE SPECULATIONS THAT IT MAY HAVE REOPENED AN ANCIENT EARTHQUAKE FAULT. DETAIL OF THE FACADE.
MIT SEINEM GEWICHT VON 700 000 TONNEN IST TAIPEI 101 SO SCHWER, DASS DARÜBER SPEKULIERT WIRD, OB ES EINE ALTE ERDBEBEN-VERWERFUNG ERNEUERT HABEN KÖNNTE.
3 THE INTERIOR SPACE THAT WAS DESIGNED ALONG *FENG SHUI* LINES.
DIE INNENRÄUME WURDE NACH FENG-SHUI-RICHTLINEN GESTALTET.

TOKYO

TOKYO

POPULATION EINWOHNERZAHL: CA. 35,000,000 INCLUDING THE GREATER
METROPOLITAN AREA INKLUSIVE METROPOLREGION
POPULATION DENSITY EINWOHNERDICHTE: 13,416 PERSONS PER KM²
AREA FLÄCHE: 621 KM² (CITY STADTZENTRUM); 5,258 KM² (METROPOLITAN AREA
METROPOLREGION)
WEBSITE: WWW.METRO.TOKYO.JP

Tokyo is the most populated urban area in the world. With over twelve million inhabitants in the city and over twenty-four million in the greater metropolitan area, this global megacity leads the way before Mexico City (22,800,000), Seoul (22,300,000), and New York City (21,900,000). The twenty-three wards that make up Tokyo have a combined population density of 13,416 persons per square kilometer. The combined nighttime population of 300,000 in the central wards of Chiyoda, Chuo, and Minato swell to over two million during the day as workers and students commute from adjacent areas. The city makes up ten percent of the country's population.

Tokio ist der am dichtesten besiedelte urbane Raum der Welt. Mit über zwölf Millionen Einwohnern im Stadtgebiet und knapp 24 Millionen in der Metropolregion rangiert die japanische Megacity vor Mexiko-Stadt (22,8 Millionen), Seoul (22,3 Millionen) und New York (21,9 Millionen). Die 23 Tokioter Bezirke weisen eine Bevölkerungsdichte von 13.416 Personen pro Quadratkilometer auf. In zentralen Bezirken wie Chiyoda, Chuo und Minato leben ständig 300.000 Menschen, tagsüber erhöht sich diese Zahl durch Berufspendler und Studenten, die aus benachbarten Regionen kommen, auf über zwei Millionen. Zehn Prozent der japanischen Bevölkerung leben in Tokio.

Tokyo has the largest metropolitan economy in the world with a nominal GDP of around US$ 1.315 trillion, which is greater than the eighth largest *national* economy of the world. The financial, political, and administrative capital of Japan, Tokyo was rated by the Economist Intelligence Unit as having the most expensive cost of living for the last fourteen years in a row. After an extended period of decline in the 1990s, Tokyo's economy has recovered, leading to renewed investment in construction from office towers to residential buildings and fashionable boutiques.

Mit einem Anteil am nominalen Bruttoinlandsprodukt von etwa 1.315 Billionen US Dollar hat Tokio die stärkste urbane Wirtschaftskraft weltweit und liegt damit sogar vor der achtgrößten nationalen Wirtschaftsmacht der Welt. Die Economist Intelligence Unit wertete Tokio, wirtschaftliche und politische Hauptstadt Japans sowie Verwaltungssitz, indessen das 14. Jahr in Folge als Stadt mit den weltweit höchsten Lebenshaltungskosten. Nach einer längeren Flaute in den 1990er Jahren hat sich die Tokioter Wirtschaft mittlerweile erholt, was unter anderem zu einer steigenden Bautätigkeit führte.

Built on bayside marshlands, Tokyo (like San Francisco) lies in one of the most earthquake-prone regions of the world. In the event of an earthquake, over ten percent of the city would turn into mush. Engineers and architects have produced buildings than can resist quakes of up to 7.2 on the Richter scale. Through the recent economic upsurge money has been poured into Tokyo's architecture with the boom in office construction followed by a surge in retail stores and luxury housing. Fashion giants have employed the likes of Herzog & de Meuron (Prada), Toyo Ito (Tod's), or Renzo Piano (Hermès) to design their outlets. In 2006 plans were announced to build a New Tokyo Tower, a 610-meter-structure that will be the tallest in the world.

Tokio wurde (wie San Francisco) auf küstennahem Schwemmland errichtet und liegt in einer der erdbebengefährdetsten Regionen der Welt – im Falle eines schweren Erdbebens würden zehn Prozent der Stadt in Schutt und Asche liegen. Architekten und Ingenieure entwickelten inzwischen Gebäudekonstruktionen, die einem Beben der Stärke 7.2 auf der Richterskala standhalten können. Der Wirtschaftsaufschwung fördert die städtebauliche und architektonische Entwicklung und begründet den Boom neuer Bürogebäude, Kaufhäuser und Luxusvillen. Modegiganten beauftragten Architekturgrößen wie Herzog & de Meuron (Prada), Toyo Ito (Tod's) oder Renzo Piano (Hermès) mit dem Entwurf von Ladengeschäften. 2006 wurde darüber hinaus bekannt gegeben, dass ein neuer Tokyo Tower gebaut werden soll, der mit 610 Metern das höchste Gebäude der Welt wäre.

DENTSU TOWER

ARCHITECTS ARCHITEKTEN: **ATELIERS JEAN NOUVEL**
YEAR OF COMPLETION FERTIGSTELLUNG: **2003**
AREA FLÄCHE: **100,000 M²**
HEIGHT HÖHE: **48 FLOORS** STOCKWERKE

A PLAY OF LIGHT

This prominent the Tokyo skyline was built by French architect Jean Nouvel, best known for his Institut du Monde Arabe in Paris, and is his first high-rise project. Built for the Japanese advertising giant Dentsu in one of the most earthquake-susceptible areas in the world, this massive steel structure consists of nearly 50 floors with over 100,000 square meters of office space, and a number of restaurants which occupy the top floor. The glass cladding and its graceful crescent shape give the building an astounding feeling of weightlessness, enhanced by the intricate gray dot pattern on every glass panel which dissolves at the edges. The inside is made up a series of stacked atria, characterized by curved and polished stainless-steel surfaces which create an interplay of light and reflection in a manner so typical for Nouvel's architecture.

LICHTSPIEL

Der Franzose Jean Nouvel, Architekt des Institut du Monde Arabe in Paris, realisierte mit dieser markante Bereicherung der Tokioter Skyline sein erstes Hochhausprojekt. Die gewaltige Stahlstruktur, die für den japanischen Werbegiganten Dentsu in einer der erdbebengefährdetsten Regionen der Welt errichtet wurde, hat annähernd 50 Stockwerke mit über 100.000 Quadratmetern Bürofläche, im obersten Geschoss befindet sich außerdem eine Reihe von Restaurants. Die von Glas geprägte Fassade und die anmutige Sichelform verleihen dem Bau eine Aura der Leichtigkeit, die durch eine besondere Behandlung der Glasoberfläche noch betont wird. Im Gebäudeinneren sind unter anderem mehrere Atrien übereinander angeordnet, die von geschwungenen und polierten Edelstahloberflächen geprägt sind. Das Material kreiert ein Wechselspiel von Licht und Schatten, wie es für Nouvels Architektur typisch ist.

1 COMPLETED IN 2003, THE DENTSU TOWER IS SITUATED IN A NEW DEVELOPMENT NEAR TOKYO STATION.
DER 2003 FERTIG GESTELLTE DENTSU TOWER LIEGT IN EINEM NEU ERSCHLOSSENEN AREAL NAHE DES HAUPTBAHNHOFS.
2 THE INTRICATE SHADING OF THE SEPARATE PANELS HAS A CONSTANTLY CHANGING EFFECT OF THE CITY'S SKYLINE.
DIE AUFWENDIGE OBERFLÄCHENBEHANDLUNG DER FASSADE SORGT FÜR SICH STÄNDIG VERÄNDERNDE EFFEKTE.
3 A VIEW INTO THE LIGHT-FILLED MAIN ATRIUM.
EIN BLICK IN DAS LICHTDURCHFLUTETE ATRIUM.

MODERN SANCTUARY

A place of repose and meditation conceals itself in the heart of Tokyo, shielded by an office space and an apartment complex: the Buddhist Baisoin Temple, one of the oldest places of worship in the city contemporarily interpreted through Kengo Kuma's new building. The temple is not just a sanctuary but also a place of meeting for the community. It offers, in its entirety, seven individual rooms for gatherings, exhibitions, music, and dance, but also for reflection. The connection between tradition and modernity is expressed in the architecture: the slanted walls of the entrance, covered with deep-ribbed metal louvers, are reminiscent of the brick roofs of the old temple. In the puritanical interior rooms, white cloth coverings that let in exterior light, allude to the traditional Japanese sliding, paper-screen doors, the so-called *shoji* screens.

MODERNES HEILIGTUM

Ein Ort der Erholung und Meditation verbirgt sich im Zentrum Tokios, abgeschirmt durch einen Büro- und Appartement-Komplex: der buddhistische Baisoin-Tempel, eine der ältesten Gebetsstätten der Stadt, modern interpretiert durch Kengo Kumas Neubau. Der Tempel ist nicht nur Heiligtum, sondern auch Treffpunkt der Gemeinde. Er bietet auf seinen insgesamt sieben Geschossen Raum für Zusammenkunft, für Ausstellungen, Musik und Tanz, aber auch für Besinnung. Die Berührungspunkte von Tradition und Gegenwart finden in der Architektur ihren Ausdruck: Die schräge Wand des Eingangsbereichs ist mit schwarzen Profilblechen verkleidet, eine Anspielung auf die Ziegeldächer der alten Tempel. In den puristischen Innenräume wirkt die weiße Stoffbespannung, durch die das Licht einfällt, wie eine Reminiszenz an die traditionellen, mit Papier bezogenen japanischen Schiebewände, die sogenannten *shoji*.

1 THE GLAZING AT THE BACK OF THE TEMPLE IS SUPPORTED BY A STRUCTURE COMPOSED OF SLENDER STEEL SLATS.
DIE VERGLASUNG AN DER TEMPELRÜCKSEITE WIRD VON EINER STRUKTUR AUS SCHLANKEN STAHLLAMELLEN GETRAGEN.
2 FROM THE ROOFTOP MEDITATION ROOM IN THE ATTIC, ONE HAS VIEWS OF THE TOKYO SKYLINE OVER THE INFINITY POOL.
VOM MEDITATIONSRAUM IM DACHGESCHOSS BLICKT MAN ÜBER DEN INFINITY POOL AUF DIE SKYLINE TOKIOS.
3 A METAL SHEAR WALL LEANS ON THE MAIN BUILDING AND PROVIDES SHELTER FOR THE ENTRANCE.
EINE METALLVERKLEIDETE WANDSCHEIBE LEHNT SICH AN DAS HAUPTGEBÄUDE UND ÜBERDACHT DEN EINGANGSBEREICH.
4 THE INTERIOR ROOMS CAPTIVATE WITH THEIR SIMPLICITY; THE FLOORS ARE COVERED WITH SLATE.
DIE INNENRÄUME BESTECHEN DURCH IHRE SCHLICHTHEIT, DIE BÖDEN SIND MIT SCHIEFER BEDECKT.

BAISOIN TEMPLE

ARCHITECTS ARCHITEKTEN: **KENGO KUMA & ASSOCIATES**
YEAR OF COMPLETION FERTIGSTELLUNG: **2003**
AREA FLÄCHE: **29,648 M²**

LEADING THE TREND

The second, free-standing Louis Vuitton fashion house in Tokyo, designed by local architect Jun Aoki, is no less stunning than it's predecessor. The luxury outfitter and leather goods icon in Tokyo's Roppongi Hills district melds into its posh surroundings without loosing its vitality. The porous facade, a monumental pixelized screen of 30,000 parallel glass tubes in honeycomb formation, is both reflective and transparent to passers-by. The storefront offers views into the interior while a complex light installation creates a mirage effect with the brand's name "Louis Vuitton" fading in and out. Louis Vuitton holds cult status in Tokyo; many of its patrons sport two bags at a time and camp out overnight in groups for store openings. The Vuitton store in Roppongi Hills remains open until 11 p.m. offering a dance floor and even a bag bar counter.

TRENDSETTER

Das freistehende Gebäude für Louis Vuitton, ein Entwurf des japanischen Architekten Jun Aoki, steht dem ersten Tokioter Bau des Modelabels an der Einkaufsstraße Omotesando in nichts nach. Die neue Boutique der Luxus-Marke im Stadtteil Roppongi vereint sich mit ihrer noblen Umgebung, ohne an Charakter zu verlieren. Die Fassade, eine große, aus 30.000 parallelen Glasröhren zusammengesetzte Fläche, die in ihrer Struktur an Bienenwaben erinnert, ist nach außen zugleich spiegelnd und transparent: Die Ladenfront ermöglicht Einblicke ins Innere, während durch eine komplexe Lichtinstallation der Markenname »Louis Vuitton« an der Schauseite lesbar wird. Der Shop in Roppongi ist bis elf Uhr abends geöffnet und bietet neben einer Tanzfläche auch eine »Bag-Bar«, an der statt Cocktails die neuesten Vuitton-Kreationen angeboten werden.

1 CLEAN, CONTEMPORARY LINES SERVE AS BACKDROP TO POWERFUL BRANDING AT ONE OF TOKYO'S MOST STYLISH ADDRESSES.
KLARE, ZEITGEMÄSSE STRUKTUREN DIENEN ALS HINTERGRUND FÜR DIE PRÄSENTATION DES MODELABELS AN EINER DER ELEGANTESTEN ADRESSEN TOKIOS.
2 MINIMALIST DÉCOR POSITION THE MERCHANDISE OPTIMALLY AND REFLECT THE EXTERIOR LINES OF THE STORE.
DIE MINIMALISTISCHE INNENAUSSTATTUNG GREIFT DIE AUSSENGESTALTUNG AUF UND LENKT DIE AUFMERKSAMKEIT AUF DIE PRODUKTE.
3 THE PATTERN FORMED BY THE EXTERIOR TUBES REFLECTS THE FAMOUS VUITTON LUGGAGE PATTERN.
DAS MUSTER, DAS DIE GLASRÖHREN DER FASSADE BILDEN, ERINNERT AN DAS BERÜHMTE VUITTON-LOGO.

LOUIS VUITTON ROPPONGI HILLS

ARCHITECTS ARCHITEKTEN: AOKI AND ASSOCIATES
YEAR OF COMPLETION FERTIGSTELLUNG: 2003

1

MAISON HERMÈS

ARCHITECTS ARCHITEKTEN: **RENZO PIANO BUILDING WORKSHOP**
WITH RENA DUMAS
YEAR OF COMPLETION FERTIGSTELLUNG: **2001**
AREA FLÄCHE: **6,071 M²**
HEIGHT HÖHE: **13 FLOORS** STOCKWERKE

RADIANT LUXURY

Renzo Piano's slender headquarters for the exclusive fashion company Hermès has been compared to a lantern glowing in the dark, much like those carried in Japanese festivals or traditionally fastened to Japanese homes. Compactly situated on a narrow site in Ginza, one of the most exclusive and expensive shopping areas in Tokyo, the building houses retail, exhibition, and office space along with a cinema and a museum devoted to the history of the company. Designed to resist earthquakes through a unique solution in which the rear columns of the seismic frame are allowed to lift off their foundations when experiencing tension, the ten-floor facade is made of specially developed glass bricks, providing it with a fashionable semi-transparency. The subway station two floors below can be directly accessed from inside the building, greatly increasing the visibility of Hermès in the public consciousness.

LEUCHTENDER LUXUS

Renzo Pianos Hauptsitz der exklusiven Modemarke Hermès gleicht einer in der Dunkelheit leuchtenden Laterne, wie sie bei japanischen Festlichkeiten getragen oder traditionell an japanischen Häusern befestigt wird. In dem Gebäude, das auf einem schmalen Grundstück in Ginza, einem der edelsten und teuersten Einkaufsviertel Tokios, errichtet wurde, befinden sich neben Verkaufsflächen, Präsentations- und Büroräumen auch ein Kino sowie ein Museum zur Geschichte des Unternehmens. Der Bau birgt darüber hinaus eine einzigartige erd-bebensichere Konstruktion, die seismische Erschütterungen dämpft. Speziell entwickelte Glasbausteine prägen die zehngeschossige Fassade und sorgen für eine elegante Semi-Transparenz. Eine unter dem Bau gelegene U-Bahn-Station, die auch vom Gebäudeinneren aus zugäng-lich ist, fördert die Erreichbarkeit des Modehauses.

1 THE MAIN COLUMNS OF THE TEN-STORY BUILDING ARE DESIGNED IN SUCH A WAY THAT THEY CAN "ROCK" DURING AN EARTHQUAKE.
DIE HAUPTSTÜTZEN DES 10-STÖCKIGEN GEBÄUDES KÖNNEN DIE ERSCHÜTTERUNGEN EINES ERDBEBENS ABFANGEN.
2 THE GLASS FACADE GLOWS LIKE A LANTERN AT NIGHT.
DIE GLASFASSADE LEUCHTET NACHTS WIE EINE LATERNE.
3 THE SEMI-TRANSPARENT GLASS BLOCKS TRANSMIT A FEELING OF UPSCALE LUXURY AND TASTE.
DIE HALBTRANSPARENTEN GLASBAUSTEINE VERMITTELN EINE LUXURIÖSE ATMOSPHÄRE.

NIHONBASHI 1-CHOME

ARCHITECTS ARCHITEKTEN: **KOHN PEDERSEN FOX ASSOCIATES**
WITH NIHON SEKKEI
YEAR OF COMPLETION FERTIGSTELLUNG: **2004**
AREA FLÄCHE: **299,618 M²**
HEIGHT HÖHE: **121 M**

ELEGANT CURVES

Nihonbashi 1-Chome, a design by the American architectural firm Kohn Petersen Fox, dominates the surrounding urban area with its 20 floors. The building complex is divided into two parts: the vertical supply channels along with the building's services are found in the northern section, encased in stone. The southern section houses extensive office space utilized by financial services firm Merrill Lynch. The amount of natural light that enters the offices can be adjusted with the use of changeable metal slats on the glass facade. The gently bowing surface of the southern facade is separated in its articulation from the mass it enclosed by deep reveals at the east and west ends to enhance its role as an independent closing layer. Furthermore, a five-story glass cube shopping area is integrated into the office section of the structure, from the west facade to the building's core and forms the link to its urban surroundings.

ELEGANTE KURVE

Nihonbashi 1-Chome, ein Entwurf des amerikanischen Architekturbüros Kohn Pedersen Fox, dominiert mit seinen 20 Stockwerken die bauliche Umgebung. Der Gebäudekomplex ist in zwei Teile gegliedert: Die vertikalen Versorgungswege sowie die Haustechnik befinden sich im Nordtrakt, dessen Fassade mit Stein verkleidet ist, der Südtrakt beherbergt großzügige Büroetagen, die von der Investmentbank Merrill Lynch genutzt werden. Der Einfall des Tageslichts in die Büroräume kann durch verstellbare Metall-Lamellen an der Glasfassade gesteuert werden. Die leicht konvex gewölbte Südfassade ist durch deutliche Tiefenversprünge an der Ost- und Westseite des Gebäudes klar vom eigentlichen Baukörper getrennt. Von der Westfassade bis zur Gebäudemitte ist außerdem ein fünfgeschossiger Glaskubus mit Verkaufsflächen in den Bürotrakt eingeschoben. Er stellt ein architektonisches Bindeglied zur urbanen Umgebung dar.

1 THE GLASS FACADE OF THE SHOPPING AREA IS EMBOSSED WITH ADDITIONAL, VERTICAL GLASS SLATS.
DIE GLASFASSADE DES LADENTRAKTS IST VON ZUSÄTZLICHEN VERTIKALEN GLASLAMELLEN GEPRÄGT.
2 THE FACADE OF THE SOUTHERN SECTION FEATURES ELEGANT CURVATURE.
DIE FASSADE DES SÜDTRAKTS WEIST EINE ELEGANTE KURVUNG AUF.
3 THE WESTERN FACADE UNITES VARIOUS BUILDING MATERIALS: STONE, GLASS, AND METAL.
DIE WESTFASSADE VEREINT DIE BAUMATERIALIEN STEIN, GLAS UND METALL.
4 THE DISTINCTIVE CURVATURE OF THE BUILDING'S SOUTHERN FACADE GIVES THE STRUCTURE AN ALMOST SCULPTURAL FEEL.
DIE MARKANTE WÖLBUNG DER SÜDFASSADE VERLEIHT DEM GEBÄUDE EINE FAST SKULPTURALE ANMUTUNG.

OPEN HOUSE

Japanese Architectural firm, Power Unit Studio, has attempted the almost impossible: to create spacious, well situated private homes in crammed, chaotic surroudings. O House built in the Meguro district of Tokyo, is just one of the private residences on architect Kei'ichi Irie's resumé. With only 50 square meters of space, he succeded in creating the illusion of size by playing with perspectives giving the home the feeling of being taller and deeper than it actually is. Much like a theater set, the space created by the sloping roof and inserted slanting walls play with the illusion of depth while the high celings provide a more spacious environment. To maintain the small budget, the same material was used throughout: reinforced concrete.

OFFENER RAUM

Das japanische Architekturbüro Power Unit Studio versucht das scheinbar Unmögliche: Es entwirft geräumige, gut gelegene Privathäuser für extrem dicht bebaute Gegenden. Eines dieser Projekte, für die Kei'ichi Irie verantwortlich zeichnet, ist O House, errichtet im Tokioter Stadtteil Meguro. Auf einem Grundstück von lediglich 50 Quadratmetern Fläche gelang es dem Architekten, durch das Spiel mit der Perspektive den Eindruck von Größe und Raum zu vermitteln. Wie bei einer Theaterbühne kreieren die schrägen Raumkonturen den Anschein von Tiefe, die hohen Decken sorgen für eine großzügige Atmosphäre. Dem begrenzten Budget entsprechend dominiert ein einziges Baumaterial: Beton.

1 A LARGE PICTURE WINDOW FILLS THE SPACE WITH NATURAL LIGHT.
EIN GROSSES PANORAMAFESTER FÜLLT DEN RAUM MIT TAGESLICHT.
2 THE BEDROOM AND BATHROOM ARE ARRANGED ON THE FIRST FLOOR WHILE THE LIVING ROOM, DINING ROOM, AND STUDY OCCUPY THE SECOND.
SCHLAF- UND BADEZIMMER BEFINDEN SICH IM ERSTEN STOCK, ESSZIMMER UND ARBEITSRAUM LIEGEN IM ZWEITEN.
3 IRIE SKEWED THE HOUSE TO FACE THE NEARBY PARK AND BUILT A LARGE WINDOW TO TAKE ADVANTAGE OF THE BEST NEIGHBORHOOD PERSPECTIVE.
IRIES ENTWURF BERÜCKSICHTIGT DEN NAHEGELEGENEN PARK, DAS GROSSE FENSTER ERMÖGLICHT DIE OPTIMALE AUSSICHT.

O-HOUSE

ARCHITECTS ARCHITEKTEN: KEI'ICHI IRIE & POWER UNIT STUDIO
YEAR OF COMPLETION FERTIGSTELLUNG: 2004
AREA FLÄCHE: 90,49 M²

PRADA EPICENTER AOYAMA

ARCHITECTS ARCHITEKTEN: **HERZOG & DE MEURO**
YEAR OF COMPLETION FERTIGSTELLUNG: **2003**
AREA FLÄCHE: **2,800M²**

STYLE PRISM

The Prada Epicenter, completed in 2003 on Tokyo's best-known fashion mile, serves as another example of luxury meets functionality. Mirroring the fashion brand's heritage of plain, simple lines, this building stands impressive amidst its older, more classical surroundings. The Swiss architects, Herzog & de Meuron, decided to play with the relationship between facade, interior walls, and shop window. These rhombuses serve as display unit, shop window, and load bearing frame all in one. Since this glass and steel exterior construction provides the support needed to hold the five-sided boutique and office space, the interior could be designed rather freely. From fur covered hangers to the snorkel-like TV screens which pipe in images, sound, and light, the shopping experience is as unique as it is luxurious.

STIL-PRISMA

Das Prada Epicenter, 2003 an Tokios bekanntester Modemeile fertig gestellt, ist ein Musterbeispiel für das Zusammentreffen von Luxus und Funktionalität. Es spiegelt die Maximen der Modemarke – klare, einfache Linien – wider und sticht eindrucksvoll aus seiner Umgebung hervor. Die Schweizer Architekten Herzog & de Meuron entwickelten ein einmaliges Zusammenspiel aus Fassade, Innenraum und Präsentationsflächen: Das Rautengerüst mit seiner Glasfüllung dient als Schaufenster, Auslage und tragendes Element gleichzeitig. Dank der Glas- und Stahlkonstruktion benötigte das fünfgeschossige Gebäude mit Verkaufsräumen und Büros keine weiteren Stützen und konnte im Inneren frei gestaltet werden. Das Epicenter bietet Design bis ins kleinste Detail: Ob pelzbedeckte Kleiderbügel oder Bildschirme, die aus den Wänden und Decken zu wachsen scheinen – das Einkaufserlebnis ist einzigartig und exquisit.

1 AT NIGHT THE STACKED FLOORS AND MERCHANDISE ARE ON DISPLAY.
NACHTS SCHEINT DAS GEBÄUDE LEUCHTEND UND TRANSPARENT.
2 REFLECTIVE BY DAY, THE BUILDING RADIATES A CALM NOT OFTEN FELT ON THE STREETS OF TOKYO.
DAS TAGESLICHT SPIEGELT SICH IN DER FASSADE UND VERLEIHT DEM GEBÄUDE EINE RUHIGE
AUSSTRAHLUNG, DIE IN DEN STRASSEN TOKIOS SELTEN IST.
3 THE DIAMOND SHAPED GLASS PANES ARE CONVEX, CONCAVE, OR FLAT AND ARE GENERALLY
TRANSPARENT EXCEPT WHEN THEY COVER DRESSING ROOMS.
DIE RAUTENFÖRMIGEN GLASSCHEIBEN SIND KONVEX, KONKAV ODER FLACH UND SIND NUR DANN
OPAK, WENN SICH ANKLEIDERÄUME DAHINTER VERBERGEN.
4 DESPITE THE DIVERSE DISPLAY METHODS, THE STORE IS POLISHED, OPEN, AND AIRY.
TROTZ DER UNTERSCHIEDLICHEN AUSLAGEN WIRKEN DIE RÄUME OFFEN UND LUFTIG.

TOD'S

ARCHITECTS ARCHITEKTEN: **TOYO ITO & ASSOCIATES**
YEAR OF COMPLETION FERTIGSTELLUNG: **2004**
HEIGHT HÖHE: **7 FLOORS** STOCKWERKE

NATURE IN CONCRETE

Toyo Ito's flagship store for the Italian brand Tod's on Tokyo's most elegant shopping boulevard, Omotesando, integrates elements from its immediate surroundings. The branching out of the numerous Zelkova trees that line the street, serve as inspiration for the net-like structure of concrete that forms the outer shell of the L-shaped building. In the 200 openings in the facade are either borderless glass plates or lined by metal sheets. The contrast between stark silhouette and organic facade, between opaque concrete and transparent glass, provides for tension and allows the store to stand out from the neighboring buildings.

MIMESE IN BETON

Toyo Itos Flagship-Store der italienischen Marke Tod's, an Tokios elegantem Einkaufsboulevard Omotesando gelegen, greift Elemente aus seiner direkten Umgebung auf. Die Verästelung der zahlreichen Zelkova-Bäume, die die Straße säumen, sind Inspiration für die netzartige Struktur aus Beton, die die äußere Hülle des L-förmigen Baus bildet. In die insgesamt 200 Durchbrüche der Fassade sind rahmenlose Fenster beziehungsweise Metallbleche eingesetzt. Der Gegensatz zwischen strenger Silhouette und organischer Fassade, zwischen opakem Beton und transparenten Glasflächen sorgt für Spannung und hebt das Gebäude deutlich von den benachbarten Bauwerken ab.

ARCHITECTS / ARCHITEKTEN

PHOTO CREDITS

© PRESTEL VERLAG, MUNICH · BERLIN · LONDON · NEW YORK 2006

© OF WORKS ILLUSTRATED BY THE ARCHITECTS AND ARTISTS,
THEIR HEIRS OR ASSIGNS, WITH THE EXCEPTION OF
© DER ABGEBILDETEN WERKE BEI DEN ARCHITEKTEN UND
KÜNSTLERN, IHREN ERBEN ODER RECHTSNACHFOLGERN MIT
AUSNAHME VON: PAUL ANDREU; REM KOOLHAAS / OFFICE FOR
METROPOLITAN ARCHITECTURE BY BEI VG BILD-KUNST, BONN 2006

FRONT COVER / UMSCHLAGVORDERSEITE: O-HOUSE, TOKYO, P. 136
P. 1: REEBOK FLAGSHIP STORE, SHANGHAI, P. 90
PP. 2–3: JIN MAO TOWER, SHANGHAI, P. 82
P. 4: HONG KONG HARBOR, P. 46
P. 144: INOTERA HEADQUARTERS, TAIPEI, P. 116
BACK COVER / UMSCHLAGRÜCKSEITE: GUANGZHOU TV &
SIGHTSEEING TOWER, P. 42

PRESTEL VERLAG
KÖNIGINSTRASSE 9, 80539 MUNICH
TEL. +49 89 381709-0
FAX +49 89 381709-35

PRESTEL PUBLISHING LTD.
4, BLOOMSBURY PLACE, LONDON WC1A 2QA
TEL. +44 20 7323-5004
FAX +44 20 7636-8004

PRESTEL PUBLISHING
900 BROADWAY, SUITE 603
NEW YORK, N.Y. 10003
TEL. +1 212 995-2720
FAX +1 212 995-2733
WWW.PRESTEL.COM

LIBRARY OF CONGRESS CONTROL NUMBER: 2006930745

BRITISH LIBRARY CATALOGUING-IN-PUBLICATION DATA

A CATALOGUE RECORD FOR THIS BOOK IS AVAILABLE FROM
THE BRITISH LIBRARY.

THE DEUTSCHE BIBLIOTHEK HOLDS A RECORD OF THIS
PUBLICATION IN THE DEUTSCHE NATIONALBIBLIOGRAFIE;
DETAILED BIBLIOGRAPHICAL DATA CAN BE FOUND UNDER:
HTTP://DNB.DDB.DE

DIE DEUTSCHE BIBLIOTHEK VERZEICHNET DIESE PUBLIKATION
IN DER DEUTSCHEN NATIONALBIBLIOGRAFIE; DETAILLIERTE
BIBLIOGRAFISCHE DATEN SIND IM INTERNET ÜBER
HTTP://DNB.DDB.DE ABRUFBAR.

PRESTEL BOOKS ARE AVAILABLE WORLDWIDE. PLEASE CONTACT
YOUR NEAREST BOOKSELLER OR ONE OF THE ABOVE ADDRESSES
FOR INFORMATION CONCERNING YOUR LOCAL DISTRIBUTOR.

PROJECT TEXTS BY PROJEKTTEXTE: NATALIE BUCHHOLZ, REEGAN
FINGER, EDGAR KROLL, CURT HOLTZ, CLAUDIA STÄUBLE

TRANSLATION OF THE PROJECT TEXTS ÜBERSETZUNGEN AUS
DEM DEUTSCHEN (PROJEKTTEXTE): JAMES RODERICK O'DONOVAN,
VIENNA WIEN

TRANSLATION OF THE ESSAY ÜBERSETZUNGEN AUS DEM
ENGLISCHEN (ESSAY): WOLFGANG HIMMELBERG, DÜSSELDORF

EDITORIAL DIRECTION PROJEKTLEITUNG: CURT HOLTZ,
CLAUDIA STÄUBLE

COPYEDITING LEKTORAT: SANDRA LEITTE

PICTURE RESEARCH BILDREDAKTION: REEGAN FINGER

COVER / LAYOUT CONCEPT UMSCHLAG / GESTALTUNGSKONZEPT:
LIQUID, AUGSBURG

DESIGN, LAYOUT, PRODUCTION GESTALTUNG, LAYOUT UND
HERSTELLUNG: WIGEL, MUNICH

ORIGINATION LITHOGRAFIE REPROLINE GENCELLER, MUNICH

PRINTED AND BOUND DRUCK UND BINDUNG: DRUCKEREI UHL,
RADOLFZELL

PRINTED IN GERMANY ON ACID-FREE PAPER

ISBN 3-7913-3683-5
978-7913-3683-1 (ENGLISH EDITION)

ISBN 3-7913-3682-7
978-3-7913-3682-4 (GERMAN EDITION)